SAP HANA Cookbook

Your all-inclusive guide to understanding SAP HANA with practical recipes

Chandrasekhar Mankala

Ganesh Mahadevan V.

PACKT PUBLISHING enterprise
professional expertise distilled

BIRMINGHAM - MUMBAI

SAP HANA Cookbook

First published: December 2013

Production Reference: 1171213

Published by Packt Publishing Ltd.
Livery Place
35 Livery Street
Birmingham B3 2PB, UK.

ISBN 978-1-78217-762-3

www.packtpub.com

Cover Image by Sandeep Vaity (sandeep.vaity@yahoo.com)

Credits

Authors
Chandrasekhar Mankala
Ganesh Mahadevan V.

Reviewers
Isaias Barroso
Mahesh Kumar CV
Kapil Ratnani

Commissioning Editor
Kunal Parikh

Acquisition Editor
Kevin Colaco

Lead Technical Editors
Mayur Hule
Arun Nadar

Technical Editors
Manan Badani
Amit Singh

Project Coordinator
Shiksha Chaturvedi

Copy Editors
Roshni Banerjee
Tanvi Gaitonde
Mradula Hegde
Aditya Nair
Adithi Shetty

Proofreaders
Ameesha Green
Paul Hindle

Indexer
Monica Ajmera Mehta

Graphics
Ronak Dhruv
Abhinash Sahu

Production Coordinator
Kyle Albuquerque

Cover Work
Kyle Albuquerque

About the Authors

Chandrasekhar Mankala is an emerging technical architect in one of the top IT firms in South-east Asia. He has more than four years of IT experience in consulting and solution architecture roles in SAP portfolios. He has been interested in SAP from the beginning of his career, and has been one of the pioneers in utilizing the SAP HANA technology since its inception.

He has worked on implementation, design, and development, and also in go-live and production in various SAP projects in niche technologies such as BW, SAP HANA, and SAP BusinessObjects over his career.

He is certified in SAP HANA and SAP BusinessObjects.

Chandra is passionate about the SAP HANA technology and its evolution and roadmap, and is always learning new tools related to SAP HANA, Big Data, and in-memory technologies.

Apart from work, he enjoys listening to music and playing video games and cricket. He can be reached at `mankala.cs@gmail.com`.

I'm very thankful to my parents for their constant prayers and blessings, which introduced me as an author to the world. I'd also like to thank my wife for supporting me during the project.

I want to thank my co-author, Ganesh, for the teamwork and co-operation throughout the project.

A big thanks to the entire Packt Publishing team—Veena, Kevin, Angel, Mayur, and Arun for guidance in the writing process. Also, big thanks to the reviewers for reviewing and providing valuable feedback.

Finally, I want to thank all my friends and colleagues, especially Srinivasrao Chandu, Venkat, and Sharath Borra for their support.

Sincere apologizes to all the people I didn't mention.

Ganesh Mahadevan V. is an adept professional in Information Technology services with nearly eight years of extensive experience in software development, delivery, solution architecting, presales consulting, and business development.

Ganesh has been the Strategic Lead for the SAP HANA technology in the South-east Asian market, and has acquired extensive expertise in collecting business requirements, conducting blueprinting workshops, customer know-how awareness, campaigns, and designing and developing applications using SAP BusinessObjects, SAP HANA, and the SAP real-time data platform.

He has relentless passion and deep expertise in data warehousing, Business Intelligence, Analytics, Big Data, and in-memory technology, and has been a speaker at various tech forums.

He has held senior positions in Analytics, IMDB, and PreSales; currently, he is a Solution Champion/Campaign Manager for the SEA ASEAN region for innovative technology—SAP HANA, SAP Real-Time Data Platform, and Analytics.

He has been involved in sales campaigns and customer workshops for CXOs with various stake holders in the region (oCXO, Business Transformation Managers, and IT heads) on SAP HANA, including real-time data platforms (Hadoop, Web Crawler, SAP HANA, Sybase IQ, SAP Data Services, and SAP BOBJ Metadata Management). He is a testing partner in various SAP products such as Lumira, Predictive Analytics, and Mobile Apps. He was involved in building solutions to GTM and played a major role in building various IS solutions.

He has maintained and strategized a persistent process in maintaining the demo landscape to discover the right business value pertaining to industries and in an innovative approach. He was the Solutions Captain for SAP HANA, SAP Real-Time Data Platform (Sybase IQ), Machine-to-Machine (M2M), and SAP BusinessObjects BI Solutions.

He lives in Bangalore with his wife and his hobbies are reading books, swimming, and politics.

I would like to acknowledge and thank the Almighty and my family members: my dad, mom, my wife, and my father-in-law for their extended support to make this book happen.

I wish to thank my co-author, who is my friend and colleague, Mr. Chandra, for his impeccable support and meticulous attitude that he carried throughout the course of authoring.

I'd also like to thank our core committee team from Packt Publishing: Angel, Shiksha, Mayur, Kevin, and the entire team for choosing us by giving us a great opportunity and their tremendous support in bringing this book to a closure.

I also want to thank my friends who extended their support and encouragement in various aspects: Venkateswarulu, Srinivas Chandu, and Prashant Kulkarni.

Last but not least, I would like to express my heartfelt gratitude to SAP for the invention of this great innovative and trendsetting technology, SAP HANA, which is not only enabling businesses with the advent of in-memory and real-time analytics, but is also going to be a pioneer in transforming businesses by harnessing its potential.

About the Reviewers

Isaias Barroso is a software architect who currently lives in Brazil. He is a specialist in high-performance and resilient software development, and he is responsible for Big Data technologies (SAP HANA, Hadoop, Pig, Hive, and so on) at the company he works for. He uses Java, Scala, and Groovy as the base programming languages for the development of projects, and he is always open to learning new programming languages that could help improve the readability and performance of code. He has architected and developed systems for many industries using different technologies over his career.

He is interested in machine learning and statistics applied on data analysis. SAP HANA is being used by him for the development of products to improve efficiency and predictive analysis for SAP HANA customers.

Mahesh Kumar CV has spent 10 years in SAP consultancy with extensive experience in the field of SAP Analytics (BW/HANA). He is a solution architect with progressive experience in design/development and consulting in SAP, specializing in SAP HANA 1.0 SP06, SAP NetWeaver Business Warehouse and BusinessObjects Reporting Tools, and especially in SAP BW/BOBJ, with subject-matter expertise in the Business Intelligence domain integrating to SAP HANA.

His experience includes end-to-end implementations, support, upgrades, and roll-up projects, as well as solution architecture and PreSales.

He is currently working as a Senior Manager in Big Data CoE at Rolta India Pvt Ltd. In the past, he has worked with CSC India Pvt Ltd, IBM India Pvt Ltd, and MindTree. His key recognitions include being a SAP mentor, SAP Topic Leader 2013 in SAP HANA Developer Center, and SAP Topic Leader 2013 in SAP HANA and In-Memory Business Data Management.

Kapil Ratnani is a software developer at SAP Labs, Bangalore, India. He holds a Master's degree in Information Technology from IIIT Bangalore. At SAP, he mainly focuses on mobile-application development and SAP HANA for backend processing. Apart from working at SAP, he has contributed to open source projects such as Notepad++, and has also launched his own open source projects such as Django_HANA and HANA SQLScript Formatter. When he is not coding, he can be found cycling around Bangalore.

www.PacktPub.com

Support files, eBooks, discount offers and more

You might want to visit www.PacktPub.com for support files and downloads related to your book.

Did you know that Packt offers eBook versions of every book published, with PDF and ePub files available? You can upgrade to the eBook version at www.PacktPub.com and as a print book customer, you are entitled to a discount on the eBook copy. Get in touch with us at service@packtpub.com for more details.

At www.PacktPub.com, you can also read a collection of free technical articles, sign up for a range of free newsletters and receive exclusive discounts and offers on Packt books and eBooks.

http://PacktLib.PacktPub.com

Do you need instant solutions to your IT questions? PacktLib is Packt's online digital book library. Here, you can access, read and search across Packt's entire library of books.

Why Subscribe?

- ▶ Fully searchable across every book published by Packt
- ▶ Copy and paste, print and bookmark content
- ▶ On demand and accessible via web browser

Free Access for Packt account holders

If you have an account with Packt at www.PacktPub.com, you can use this to access PacktLib today and view nine entirely free books. Simply use your login credentials for immediate access.

Instant Updates on New Packt Books

Get notified! Find out when new books are published by following @PacktEnterprise on Twitter, or the *Packt Enterprise* Facebook page.

Table of Contents

Preface   **1**

Chapter 1: SAP HANA Studio – Look and Feel   **5**

Introduction   5
Understanding SAP HANA Studio   5
Switching between different views – perspectives   7
Navigating SAP HANA Studio – the Navigator Pane   10
Administering SAP HANA – the Administration Console perspective   15
Modeling SAP HANA Studio – the Modeler perspective   22

Chapter 2: Data Provisioning   **25**

Introduction   25
Loading data into SAP HANA – data provisioning methods   26
Uploading data from flat files   31
Using SLT to load data into SAP HANA   41
Using SAP Data Services as an ETL tool to load data into SAP HANA   55
Loading data into SAP HANA using DXC   70
Loading data using SAP Sybase Replication Server   75

Chapter 3: Modeling   **83**

Introduction   83
Approaching SAP HANA modeling   83
Creating attribute views   85
Creating analytic views   90
Creating calculation views   94
Preparing documents – Auto Documentation   110
Modeling with Information Composer   113

Chapter 4: Reporting — 121

Introduction — 121
The reporting layer on top of SAP HANA — 122
Connecting reporting tools to SAP HANA — 123
Creating reports using SAP BusinessObjects Web Intelligence — 128
Creating reports using SAP BusinessObjects Explorer — 142
Creating reports using SAP BusinessObjects Dashboards/Xcelsius — 148
Creating reports using SAP BusinessObjects Analysis for OLAP — 154
Creating reports using Microsoft Excel — 158
Creating reports in SAP Lumira — 165

Chapter 5: Advanced Features in SAP HANA — 171

Introduction — 171
Converting different currencies — 172
Creating hierarchies — 174
Creating variables — 177
Creating input parameters — 179
Creating filters — 182
Creating procedures using SQLScript — 184
Creating decision tables — 185

Chapter 6: User Management — 189

Introduction — 189
Creating users — 189
Creating roles — 192
Assigning roles to users — 193
Restricting access to data – creating analytic privileges — 195
Securing logging in to SAP HANA – authentication methods — 200
Securing logging in to SAP HANA – privileges — 202

Appendix A: Introduction to SAP HANA — 205

Introduction — 205
Explaining traditional databases and bottlenecks — 206
Introducing technology and hardware innovations — 211
Looking into versions and technical requirements — 216
Describing why you should use SAP HANA — 220
Looking into SAP HANA features — 224
Comparing BWA and SAP HANA — 228

Appendix B: Architecture   231

  Understanding the SAP HANA architecture   231

  Explaining IMCE and its components   234

  Storing data – row storage   239

  Storing data – column storage   243

  Understanding the persistence layer   247

  Understanding backup and recovery   249

Appendix C: Applications Powered by SAP HANA   253

  Introduction   253

  Introducing flavors on top of SAP HANA   253

  Introducing SAP NetWeaver BW powered by SAP HANA   254

  Introducing SAP Business Suite on SAP HANA   256

Index   259

Preface

SAP HANA (High-Performance Analytical Appliance) is an in-memory, column store database that supports real-time data loads and analytics. As the name conveys, SAP HANA is an appliance combining hardware and software. SAP has been providing business applications for different domains for many years. Now, it has come up with a game-changing database platform that helps a business to run faster and analyze decision-making in real time, thus helping users to analyze data within seconds.

In SAP HANA, both analytical and transactional data is stored. Along with this, analysis of the data combination is possible on-the-fly. SAP HANA unleashes the potential to analyze Big Data in real time, which includes structured and unstructured data. SAP HANA also supports data warehousing in which existing SAP NetWeaver Business Warehouse (SAP BW) models to SAP HANA and makes decisions on top of this. SAP HANA also possesses libraries that support predictive, spatial, and textual analysis, which can be run on multiple data sources.

What this book covers

Chapter 1, SAP HANA Studio – Look and Feel, gives an introduction to SAP HANA Studio, the GUI which will be used throughout the book for almost all the recipes.

Chapter 2, Data Provisioning, provides recipes on how to load data into SAP HANA using different tools. The source system for the data can be either SAP or non-SAP systems. Moreover, as SAP HANA supports real-time analysis, a selection of tools and the types of data load will also be covered. Recipes in this chapter help in deciding on and implementing the solutions.

Chapter 3, Modeling, shows how to create models in SAP HANA. The models created will be exposed for reporting. Once we have data in physical tables, we create models in SAP HANA that help us to analyze data on-the-fly.

Chapter 4, Reporting, shows how to create reports on top of SAP HANA models and consume data for analysis. Different people in the organization use the same data in different ways for their analysis. Recipes in this chapter will help us learn how to do analysis using different reporting tools on top of SAP HANA.

Chapter 5, Advanced Features in SAP HANA, helps you learn how to work with advanced features such as hierarchies and currency conversion in SAP HANA. The recipes in this chapter may not be useful in all situations, but they help in complex scenarios.

Chapter 6, User Management, introduces the basics of administration in SAP HANA, which covers user role creation, assigning them, and how they work.

Appendix A, Introduction to SAP HANA, gives a basic idea of what SAP HANA is by describing the features and comparing it with traditional databases available on the market.

Appendix B, Architecture, explains the core architecture in detail with all the components of SAP HANA.

Appendix C, Applications Powered by SAP HANA, shows how SAP HANA can be used as a database in supporting other applications.

What you need for this book

There are different SAP HANA editions offered by SAP. We need to have any one edition installed:

Software component	Enterprise edition extended	Enterprise edition	Platform edition
HANA Studio	X	X	X
HANA Information Composer	X	X	X
HANA Client	X	X	X
HANA Client for Excel	X	X	X
HANA User Interface for information access	X	X	X
HANA Database	X	X	X
HANA Host Agent	X	X	X
Diagnostics Agent	X	X	X
BusinessObjects Data Services	X	X	
HANA Direct Extractor Connection (DXC)	X	X	
Landscape Transformation Add-on (SLT)	X	X	
Landscape Transformation Replication Server	X	X	
HANA Load Controller (LC)	X		

Software component	Enterprise edition extended	Enterprise edition	Platform edition
Sybase Replication Server and Agent	X		
Sybase Adaptive Server Enterprise (ASE)	X		

Who this book is for

If you are a beginner and you consider yourself as a future SAP HANA modeler, then this is the perfect book for you. You should have basic knowledge of RDBMS concepts and SQL to start preparing the recipes that are covered in this book.

Conventions

In this book, you will find a number of styles of text that distinguish between different kinds of information. Here are some examples of these styles, and an explanation of their meaning.

Code words in text, database table names, folder names, filenames, file extensions, pathnames, dummy URLs, user input, and Twitter handles, are shown as follows: "These jobs will be recreated automatically from `IUUC_MONITOR_<mass_transfer_id>`."

A block of code is set as follows:

```
Var_out = SELECT "SalesOrderId","ProductId","QuantityUnit","Currenc
y","Quantity","GrossAmount","NetAmount" from "_SYS_BIC"."SAP_HANA_
COOKBOOK/AN_SAP_HANA_COOKBOOK";
```

Words that you see on the screen, in menus or dialog boxes for example, appear in the text like this: "Enter the values for SAP HANA **Hostname** and **Instance Number**, and then click on **Next**."

Reader feedback

Feedback from our readers is always welcome. Let us know what you think about this book—what you liked or may have disliked. Reader feedback is important for us to develop titles that you really get the most out of.

To send us general feedback, simply send an e-mail to `feedback@packtpub.com`, and mention the book title via the subject of your message.

If there is a topic that you have expertise in and you are interested in either writing or contributing to a book, see our author guide on `www.packtpub.com/authors`.

Customer support

Now that you are the proud owner of a Packt book, we have a number of things to help you to get the most from your purchase.

Errata

Although we have taken every care to ensure the accuracy of our content, mistakes do happen. If you find a mistake in one of our books—maybe a mistake in the text or the code—we would be grateful if you would report this to us. By doing so, you can save other readers from frustration and help us improve subsequent versions of this book. If you find any errata, please report them by visiting http://www.packtpub.com/submit-errata, selecting your book, clicking on the **errata submission form** link, and entering the details of your errata. Once your errata are verified, your submission will be accepted and the errata will be uploaded on our website, or added to any list of existing errata, under the Errata section of that title. Any existing errata can be viewed by selecting your title from http://www.packtpub.com/support.

Piracy

Piracy of copyright material on the Internet is an ongoing problem across all media. At Packt, we take the protection of our copyright and licenses very seriously. If you come across any illegal copies of our works, in any form, on the Internet, please provide us with the location address or website name immediately so that we can pursue a remedy.

Please contact us at copyright@packtpub.com with a link to the suspected pirated material.

We appreciate your help in protecting our authors, and our ability to bring you valuable content.

Questions

You can contact us at questions@packtpub.com if you are having a problem with any aspect of the book, and we will do our best to address it.

1
SAP HANA Studio – Look and Feel

In this chapter, we will cover:

- ▶ Understanding about SAP HANA Studio
- ▶ Switching between different views – perspectives
- ▶ Navigating SAP HANA Studio – the Navigator Pane
- ▶ Administering SAP HANA Studio – the Administration Console perspective
- ▶ Modeling SAP HANA Studio – the Modeler perspective

Introduction

This chapter discusses SAP HANA Studio. It covers the technology used in developing the SAP HANA Studio interface, how to navigate the different options available, the operations supported, and so on.

Understanding SAP HANA Studio

This recipe introduces you to why and where SAP HANA Studio is used. We will also look at how SAP HANA Studio has been developed and the technologies used behind its development.

How it works...

SAP HANA Studio runs on the Eclipse platform and is both the central development environment and the main administration tool for SAP HANA. SAP HANA Studio is used by administrators to administer activities, such as to start and stop services, monitor the system, configure system settings, and manage users and authorizations. SAP HANA Studio interacts with the servers of the SAP HANA database by using SQL. Developers use SAP HANA Studio for content creation such as information views and stored procedures. These development objects are stored in the SAP HANA repository. SAP HANA Studio is developed in the Java language and is based on the Eclipse platform.

SAP HANA Studio is the interface between the HANA database and the reporting layer or the HANA database and the presentation layer. It is the area where we design our models (for example, data models—3NF, 5NF, dimension models—based on star schema where we have facts, dimensions, and so on). SAP HANA Studio is a collection of applications for the SAP HANA appliance software. It enables developers, modelers, or technical users to work on development activities of the SAP HANA database. These activities include creating/managing user authorizations and building models, which can be creating new or editing existing models of data in the SAP HANA database. SAP HANA Studio is a client environment which can be used to access the SAP HANA database. The database can be located in the same environment or at a remote location.

There's more...

Platforms supported

SAP HANA Studio runs on the Eclipse platform Version 3.6. SAP HANA Studio can be used on the following platforms:

- Microsoft Windows x32 and x64 versions of XP, Vista, and Windows 7
- 64-bit versions of the Linux platform such as SUSE and Ubuntu
- For Mac OS X, SAP HANA Studio (Version 1.00.60) is available for download

System requirements

Java JRE 1.6 or 1.7 must be installed to run SAP HANA Studio. The path variable parameters have to be set for JRE. The correct Java variant installation has to be selected accordingly, 32 bit or 64 bit.

Installation paths

An installation path has to be defined while installing, otherwise default values will be applied, as shown:

 ▸ Microsoft Windows 32 bit (x86): `C:\Program Files (x86)\sap\hdbstudio`

 ▸ Linux 64 bit (x86): `/usr/sap/hdbstudio`

 ▸ Microsoft Windows 32 bit: `C:\Program Files\sap\hdbstudio`

 ▸ Microsoft Windows 64 bit: `C:\Program Files\sap\hdbstudio`

See also

 ▸ Eclipse IDE at `http://en.wikipedia.org/wiki/Eclipse_(software)`

Switching between different views – perspectives

We use the same IDE, SAP HANA Studio, for different activities, such as modeling, administration, and transports. The corresponding perspective has to be set to perform these respective activities. This recipe explains in detail about the perspectives available.

Getting ready

SAP HANA Studio presents its various tools in the form of perspectives.

A perspective contains specific task- or resource-related functions. It determines which views and editors are available and controls what appears in certain menus and toolbars for the developers, modelers, or technical users to leverage based on the requirements.

Database administration and monitoring features are contained primarily within the **Administration Console** perspective. There are other perspectives as well, which include **Modeler**, **SAP HANA Development**, **Debug**, and **Lifecycle Management**, as shown in the following screenshot:

How it works...

There are several key Eclipse perspectives that you will use while developing; however, these are the major ones that are used predominantly:

- **Modeler**: The Modeler perspective is used to define information models and to create various types of views and analytical privileges to create models. It allows users to create new or modify existing models of data. Modelers can create different types of models (for example, attribute views, analytic views, and calculation views) depending on the data, which can be transaction data, master data, or any dimensional or other data. All databases are listed in the Navigator Pane of the studio.

- **SAP HANA Development**: This perspective consists of new tools specifically created for SAP HANA XS (Extended Application Services). These tools help in writing the server-side JavaScript code. This perspective is used to create development objects that access or update models. There are native and non-native applications that are supported, such as JScript, HTML5, Java, and .Net.

- ▶ **Debug**: This perspective is used for debugging purposes, such as server-side JavaScript or SQLScript.

- ▶ **Administration Console**: This perspective is used to monitor the system and change settings. This perspective allows administrators to administer and monitor the SAP HANA database instances. It also includes the database status information. Administrators can check the overview of the system, servers, running services, diagnose logfiles, monitor log size, volume size, system performance, multiple alerts, and so on. They can also create users and roles and can assign privileges to roles.

- ▶ **Lifecycle Management**: This perspective is used for future releases and upgrades. It helps in providing automated updates for SAP HANA using SAP Software Update Manager.

How to do it...

From the **Window** menu, select **Open Perspective** and change the perspective accordingly. At the bottom of the menu, we can see the **Other** option, from where we can access other perspectives as well, as shown in the following screenshot:

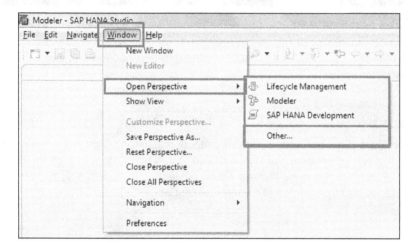

In the top-right corner of SAP HANA Studio, we have an option to open the available perspectives and change them.

By clicking on the ⬚ icon, we can navigate between perspectives.

There's more...

The previously mentioned perspectives are the most frequently used. Other than these, we have another perspective, which is the **PlanViz** perspective. This perspective is used when we use the visualize plan for an SQL code.

See also

- ▶ The **Plugin** perspective
- ▶ The **Resource** perspective
- ▶ The **JavaScript** perspective
- ▶ The **Team Synchronizing** perspective

Navigating SAP HANA Studio – the Navigator Pane

When we log on to SAP HANA Studio, this is the place through which we can access all the objects—schemas, tables, procedures, information views, and so on. We can see this pane on the left side of the studio. This recipe discusses the different actions that can be performed from the **Navigator Pane**.

Getting ready

SAP HANA Studio is client software deployed on local machines which is used to connect to the SAP HANA server (database). For this, we have to add the system with all the details in the Navigator Pane. It is this pane that we will be navigating to access objects in the database and achieve tasks, as shown in the following screenshot:

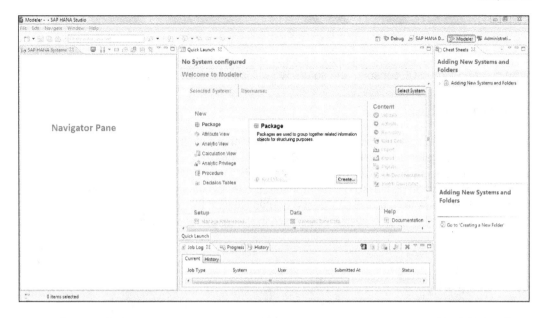

At first look, the pane looks empty as we don't have any systems added. Once we add systems, we can browse through all the content. We can connect to multiple HANA databases from a single studio. Let us say that, a company has multiple HANA servers across the landscape—Development, Quality, and Production. Individual entries have to be added for each system and connected to the same.

The options in the Navigator Pane depend on the opened perspective. When we are in the Modeler perspective, we will see only the available systems and the objects. The content differs with the SAP HANA Development perspective or Debug perspective. This can be seen in the following screenshot:

How it works...

There are other options in the top portion of the Navigator Pane to monitor system health, administration, the SQL console, and so on. We will look at all the available options in detail.

System Monitor

We can monitor the system using the ⊞ option. When we click on this button, details of all the available systems will be displayed. By default, information available in the memory, used memory, and so on will be displayed system wise. These results can be configured with what data needs to be displayed on the monitor screen. We can further drill down to the administration mode from this menu. Just a double-click on the system will take us to the administration section of that system, as shown in the following screenshot:

Administration

The ⚙ ▼ option helps us with the administration of a particular system. More details on this option will be covered in the *Administering SAP HANA – the Administration Console perspective* recipe of this chapter.

As we deal with the administration of the system, this completely depends on the roles and authorizations we possess in the system.

SQL Console

The SQL option opens up an SQL console, where we can write the SQL code for different purposes. We usually write the SQL code for DDL/DML/TCL operations, such as creating/altering a table, inserting/updating/previewing/deleting data contents of a table, or committing updates. The code written in this is reusable. We can save the code as a file on our local PC and use the same code in the future.

The SQL code will be executed based on the roles/authorizations we have on a system. We should have authorization to execute SQL on a schema; otherwise, the execution fails with an invalid authorization issue. The **SQL Console** window is as shown in the following screenshot:

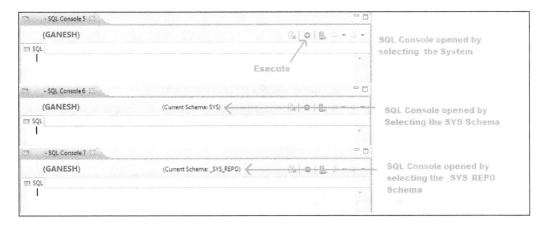

The level we select while opening the SQL console is very important. As shown in the preceding screenshot, we can see the name of the schema for which the SQL console has been opened. Text in the header section of the SQL console will be in the following format:

```
SYSTEM_NAME (USER_NAME) HOST_NAME (Current Schema: SCHEMA_NAME)
```

Let's have a look at each of the fields:

- SYSTEM_NAME: This represents the system which has been selected for opening SQL Console. The length of the system name will be three characters.
- USER_NAME: This tells us the username with which we have logged in to the system and are working with in SQL Console.
- HOST_NAME: This shows the details of the host to which we are connected. The same host details can be seen from the properties of the system.
- SCHEMA_NAME: This gives us the name of the schema which has been selected while opening the SQL Console window. If SQL Console has been opened while selecting the system, we don't see this in the header section. From the preceding screenshot, we can see that when SQL Console is opened from the system level, no schema details are displayed. The same happens when we select a schema and open SQL Console; we can see the schema on which SQL Console is working.

The important thing here is that when we execute any SQL command without giving a schema name, it works on the schema which we have selected. When tables/views are created without giving the schema name, these will go and sit in the schema. There is no restriction on fetching data from any schema; we can run SQL on any schema to retrieve data.

Find Table

The 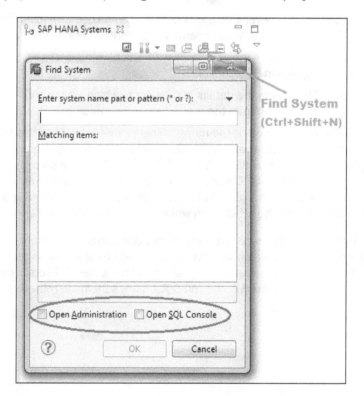 option helps us in searching for a table in the system. This icon will be active only when we select a catalog folder in the system, as tables will be located in the catalog section. Even though a schema is selected to find a table, the search will be executed on the entire system. All the tables with the given search string will be returned. We can also select to include column names in the search. In this case, results will consist of the column names as well. The minimum length of the search string is two characters.

Find System

The option can be used to search systems. The name of the system will be stored in the following format:

```
SYSTEM_NAME    HOST_NAME    (USER_NAME)
```

A search will be executed soon after giving a single character. A search string can be a part of the system name, host name, or a username. All values that match will be displayed. There are two more options, **Open Administration** and **Open SQL Console,** at the bottom of the search window, as shown in the following screenshot. If these are checked, it automatically opens the corresponding windows—Administration/SQL Console.

Link with Editor

The ⇆ option links the objects opened with the navigation pane. When this option is enabled and an object is selected, the corresponding object in the navigation pane will be highlighted automatically. For example, let us assume that we are working on a few tables, views, and procedures opened in SQL Console, which are present in different schemas. When we change from one object to another in the main window, the same object in the respective schema will be highlighted in the navigation pane. This allows us to search where the objects are located exactly when required.

There's more...

> ▸ Cheat sheets can be opened in SAP HANA Studio. Select the **Window** menu, expand **Show View** and select **Other**. Now expand the **Help** folder. We can see **Cheat Sheets**. Select it, now we can see the Cheat Sheets pane on the right-hand side of SAP HANA Studio

> ▸ Views in SAP HANA Studio

See also

> ▸ *SAP HANA Database – Studio Installation and Update Guide* at `http://help.sap.com/hana/SAP_HANA_Studio_Installation_Update_Guide_en.pdf`

Administering SAP HANA – the Administration Console perspective

This recipe introduces another perspective. This perspective is more helpful for administrative purposes.

Getting ready

The Administration Console perspective helps with the administration aspects of SAP HANA. This perspective is helpful for SAP HANA technology users (database administrators) who work on regular administrative tasks which involve maintaining and monitoring system status, monitoring disk volume usage, configuring alerts, and so on.

Let us go through the different options in this perspective. The following screenshot illustrates the Administration Console perspective:

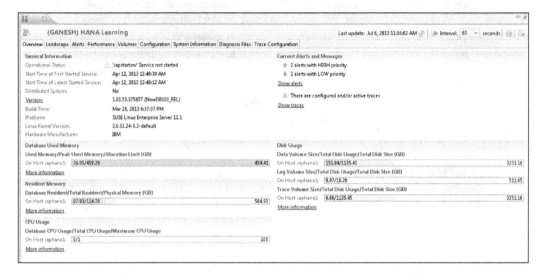

How to do it...

We need to configure a system in SAP HANA Studio before starting to work on it. There could be different systems available in the landscape—Development, Quality, and Production. The following is the process of adding a system.

Adding a system

In order to connect to a SAP HANA instance, we need to know the server credentials and details (user ID, server, password, and instance number). The left-hand side of the studio Navigator Pane shows the available HANA instances in SAP HANA Studio. Following are the steps to add a new system:

1. Right-click in the Navigator space and click on **Add System**, as shown in the following screenshot:

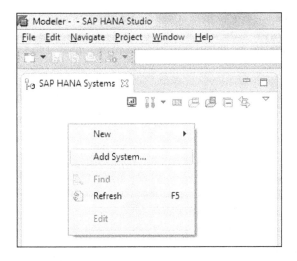

2. Enter the values for SAP HANA **Hostname** and **Instance Number** and then click on **Next**, as shown in the following screenshot:

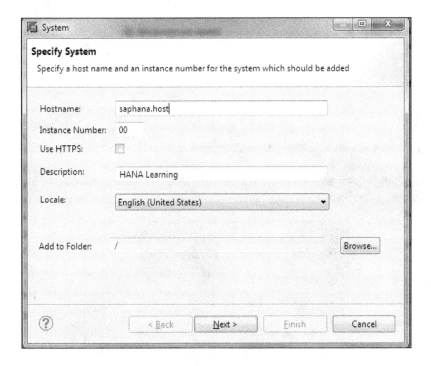

3. Enter the database credentials—**User Name** and **Password**—to connect to the SAP HANA database. After the successful connection to SAP HANA, click on **Next** and then click on **Finish**, as shown in the following screenshot:

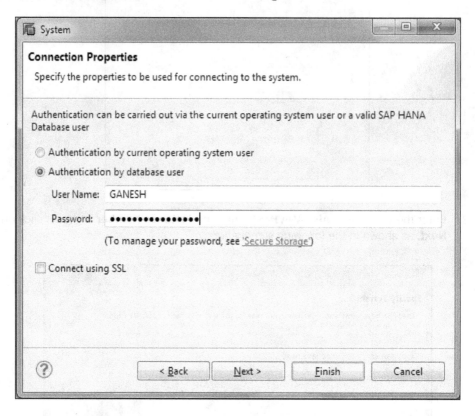

4. The SAP HANA system now appears in the Navigator Pane, as shown in the following screenshot:

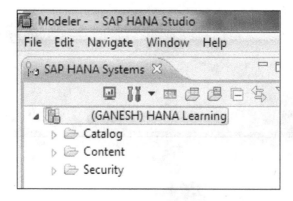

There's more...

Apart from adding a system, there are other activities as well that can be done in the **Administration Console** perspective.

Overview

In this tab, we can have a snapshot of the overall status of the system. As shown in the screenshot in the *Getting ready* section of this recipe, it includes the system status, build version, hardware and software details, disk memory utilization, CPU utilization, and so on. We can dive into each category to get in-depth details.

Landscape

In the **Landscape** menu, we can have a glance at different services running and their administration, configuring hosts, redistribution operation on tables, and so on.

Services

Under this category, activities related to services are handled. All the services running across every host will be available here. We can start, stop, or kill the services. Memory usage and allocation details across different servers can be monitored, and the result set can be customized by fields to be displayed.

Configuration

Hosts can be configured using **Configuration**. Assignment details of master/slaves for all servers can be monitored from this screen.

Redistribution Operations

Tables have to be redistributed among index servers for effective utilization of resources and optimal performance. Performance will be optimal when frequently joined tables are located in the same index server compared to those that are spread into different index servers. Therefore, it is highly recommended to distribute the tables among index servers. This can be performed soon after adding the hosts or later as well based on the models we build on the tables, for which we have separate options available.

The same operation has to be applied for partitioned tables as well. Partitioned tables will be distributed across different index servers. This location can be specified manually or determined by the database when it has been partitioned initially. The size of these partitions will be growing in time, which may not give us optimal results. Therefore, it is required to redistribute the partition tables as well.

Alerts

For an administrator, system status, services, and resources have to be monitored continuously. Configuring alerts will help in making timely decisions. In the generation of alerts, the statistics server plays a major role. When the SAP HANA system is started, the statistics server is automatically activated on the host of the active master name server. The statistics server runs SQL commands internally and collects all the information from all index servers. From this data, important alerts information will be displayed in the **Overview** tab and the **Alerts** tab will hold detailed level data.

E-mail notifications can be configured for these alerts and thereby all stakeholders will be updated on alerts. The sender's e-mail address, recipient's e-mail address, and SMTP port details are required for this setting. The recipients listed will be notified by e-mail upon generation of alerts by the statistics server.

Performance

All performance-related processes can be monitored from this tab. This includes threads, sessions, SQL cache, expensive statements, progress in jobs, load details, and so on.

Whenever there is an I/O operation in the SAP HANA system, it starts threads on the corresponding server. The detailed level of data on these threads can be monitored and can be cancelled if required. Similarly, details related to open sessions, SQL plan cache, expensive statements executed, and jobs which are progressing can be monitored.

Apart from these, the load impact on the SAP HANA system can be monitored. Flexible options are provided to change the filters dynamically so that we can drill down or drill up on the data of any server in the host. This really helps in understanding where the server is being impacted with peak loads on which server.

It makes no sense if system resources are not effectively utilized after taking on a powerful, in-memory database such as SAP HANA.

Volumes

The **Volumes** tab gives us complete detail on the memory statistics of all servers (name server, index server, statistics server, and XS Engine) on the host. This includes total disk size, used disk size, remaining disk size, and volume size. Details about data volumes, log volumes along with the page size, and block size are also available.

Configuration

The **Configuration** tab has highly sensitive data as all the system configurations are maintained in this section. For the SAP HANA system, configurations are stored in the form of configuration files—the `.ini` files. We will have several values, and these settings can be changed for the host or the entire system. When the value is changed, a green mark will be shown indicating changed values. Against a few values, a minus sign will be displayed. We cannot change these values and they are set by the system itself, as shown in the following screenshot:

System Information

The **System Information** tab holds the system information table, which has data related to the SAP HANA system. Data in each table can be viewed and a detailed analysis can be performed to take decisions for system maintenance. This includes tables on memory consumption, work load statistics, transactions in use, and many more.

Diagnosis Files

Trace and logfiles of the system can be browsed from this menu (all the trace and logfiles right from the starting date of the system setup). These files can be viewed or downloaded to a local PC.

Trace Configuration

Detailed information about the actions of the HANA database can be obtained using different traces. We can activate these traces and configure them as per our requirements.

We can configure the following traces:

S No	Trace	Default Configuration
1	SQL trace	Inactive
2	Performance trace	Inactive
3	Kernel profiler trace	Inactive
4	Global database trace	Active with default trace level ERROR
5	Database trace	Active with default trace level ERROR
6	User-specific trace	Not specified
7	End-to-end trace	Active with default trace level ERROR
8	Expensive statements trace	Inactive

See also

▶ *SAP HANA Administration Guide* at `http://help.sap.com/hana/SAP_HANA_Administration_Guide_en.pdf`

Modeling SAP HANA Studio – the Modeler perspective

In this recipe, we will see how a modeler starts working in SAP HANA Studio to accomplish modeling activities. To perform any modeling activity, we have to switch to the Modeler perspective.

Getting ready

All the modeling activities will be done from this perspective. We will be creating tables, information views, SQL procedures, and so on. Let us talk in brief about this perspective.

How it works...

SAP HANA Modeler is a graphical data modeling tool used to design analytical models and analytical privileges. Analytical models are used to load data and report on top of them, whereas analytical privileges are used to restrict access to those models. SAP HANA Modeler is intended for users with extensive technical knowledge and can therefore be regarded as the more powerful tool. The Modeler perspective supports functions as shown:

- ▸ Creating information views (attribute/analytic/calculation) and analytic privileges
- ▸ Processing models
- ▸ Administration tasks such as managing modeling content
- ▸ Importing table definitions/schemas
- ▸ Loading data

The Modeler perspective is as shown in the following screenshot:

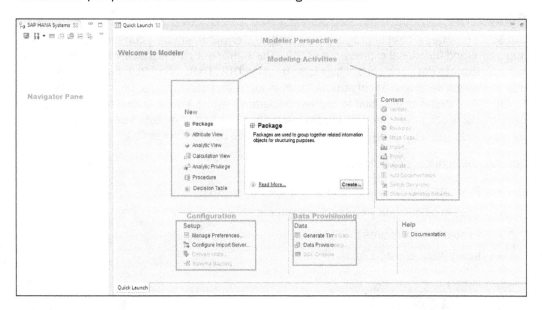

There's more...

In the modeling section of SAP HANA, there are several things to know. A few of them are explained in this recipe.

Information views

Information views are of different types—**Attribute View**, **Analytic View**, and **Calculation View**. When we use an information composer, a calculation view is created. Calculation views are basically a query which is built on top of analytic views and other calculation views to meet a complex business requirement.

Some of the features are as follows:

- ▸ Attribute views
- ▸ Analytic views
- ▸ Calculation views
- ▸ Transportable design time objects are stored in the repository
- ▸ Database objects (column store views) are generated from these development artifacts

SQLScript

SQLScript provides a flexible programming language environment as a combination of imperative and functional expressions of SQL. The significant part is that it allows developers to easily express data and control flow logic by using DDL, DML, and SQL query statements as well as imperative language constructs, such as loops and conditionals. On the other hand, functional expressions are used to express declarative logic for the efficient execution of data-intensive computations. This logic is internally represented as data flow, which can be executed in parallel as SAP HANA supports massive parallel processing.

Some of the features are as follows:

- ▸ Push data-intensive operations into the SAP HANA database
- ▸ Used in calculation views and procedures
- ▸ Read-only procedures
- ▸ Read/Write procedures

See also

- ▸ *SAP HANA Modeling Guide* at `http://help.sap.com/hana/SAP_HANA_Modeling_Guide_en.pdf`

2
Data Provisioning

In this chapter, we will cover:

- ▸ Loading data into SAP HANA – data provisioning methods
- ▸ Uploading data from flat files
- ▸ Using SLT to load data into SAP HANA
- ▸ Using SAP Data Services as an ETL tool to load data into SAP HANA
- ▸ Loading data into SAP HANA using DXC
- ▸ Loading data using Sybase Replication Server

Introduction

The process of loading data into SAP HANA is called data provisioning. There are many ways to load data into the SAP HANA system. We can use several available tools for data provisioning. The decision to select an appropriate tool depends on the requirement and other factors, such as the type of source system, the complexity of data transformations required between the source system and SAP HANA, and whether the replication is real time or not.

In this chapter, we will see the different tools and options that are available for data provisioning: loading data from flat files, using SAP Data Services, SAP Landscape Transformation, and Sybase Replication techniques.

Loading data into SAP HANA – data provisioning methods

Based on the requirements, the data provisioning methods for loading data into SAP HANA are different. This recipe briefs you on the tools available for data provisioning and how they work.

Getting ready

This recipe briefs you on the tools available for data provisioning and its application.

How to do it...

The process of data loading is different for the data provisioning tools. In this recipe, we will see in detail the technique and options available for loading data into SAP HANA using different tools. The next recipes deal individually with each tool.

How it works...

As mentioned earlier, the selection of a data provisioning tool depends on the characteristics of the source system and other factors. The mechanism of each data provision technique differs. Let us look at the key factors in each technique that will help in deciding which mechanism to select. Here, the key factors will only be discussed for SLT, SAP DS, and Sybase replication, as loading flat files is just a simple import of file into the SAP HANA system.

SAP Landscape Transformation

SAP Landscape Transformation (**SLT**) is a trigger-based replication technique. This is the primarily used technique for provisioning of data from the SAP system. The following are the key factors to be considered while selecting SLT as the data provisioning mechanism:

- The SLT server has to be installed separately.
- Real-time replication of data is possible. If there is a requirement for real-time data replication from a source system, this is the technique.
- This works by capturing changes made to the tables on the source side by detecting the triggers sent by the database to update tables. When there are changes to the data in tables, they are replicated to SAP HANA.
- We can schedule the replication as a real-time or batch process, and it can be periodic.

- ▸ Data and metadata from tables can be replicated using this technique.

- ▸ Selective replication of data is possible by applying filters and selecting only the fields that need to be replicated.

- ▸ SLT can also be used to load data from non-SAP source systems. The source database must meet some criteria to support the replication server that captures the changes.

SAP Data Services

The SAP **Data Services** (**DS**) technique is implemented in most of the cases. While replicating data using this mechanism, the following key factors should be noted:

- ▸ A separate software component, SAP Data Services, is required and has to be installed

- ▸ Replication is done by scheduling jobs batch-wise, say hourly or daily

- ▸ Both data and metadata from tables can be replicated to SAP HANA

- ▸ Complex transformations and data cleansing are possible

- ▸ The replication can leverage existing extractors, function modules, and programs in the source system

- ▸ Data loading from non-SAP source systems is also possible

Sybase replication

This replication technique is a log-based replication. It is specific to non-SAP systems, databases, and so on; for example, ASE, Oracle, MS SQL, and DB2 UDB on Linux, Unix, and Windows (LUW). The key factors for this replication technique are as follows:

- ▸ Sybase replication uses database log tables to identify changes in the source system. Hence, this will be carried at the database level.

- ▸ In this replication, the application layer is bypassed. Hence, it is a high-performing, real-time replication mechanism.

- ▸ Filtering or transformation of data is not possible as the application layer is not involved in the replication. Hence, the mapping will be one-to-one and at the table level.

- ▸ An exact copy of the data in the source table is replicated into SAP HANA.

- ▸ It supports real-time data replication from non-SAP systems.

Considering all these features and the key points under each replication technique, it is clear that these data provision mechanisms differ functionally and technically. Based on the business requirement, a solution has to be built selecting one of the preceding data provisioning techniques.

There's more...

We have to think about strategic and technical considerations while deciding the exact data provisioning technique. We will discuss these briefly.

Strategic considerations

First we must understand the operational and corporate requirements. For this, there are certain factors to be considered. These are listed as follows:

- Real-time replication or non real-time replication of data
- Source system
- Type of data—transactional, hierarchical, unstructured, and so on
- Complexity of transformations

While understanding these requirements and answering these points, we will come across different situations such as different source systems—SAP, non-SAP, disk-based legacy databases, external files in the form of CSV (comma-delimited files), and unstructured data; and the data provisioning tool will be preferred accordingly. For example, in the case of unstructured data, SAP Data Services is preferred as cleansing of data will be required prior to loading. If data is available in the form of external files, we may not need any tool; data from files can be directly imported to SAP HANA using SAP HANA Studio. If required, we can also use SAP Data Services to load from files. If real-time data replication is required, SLT is preferred as this helps in loading up-to-the-minute data from all source systems that are compatible with SLT, thereby maximizing the availability of updated data to the end users. When huge transformations and data cleansing is required, we go with SAP Data Services.

Technical considerations

On the other hand, technical considerations also have to be taken into account before deciding on the replication tool. This includes the following factors:

- Data replication capabilities
- Source system compatibility
- Administration/configuration aspects

The following table gives a clear picture of the entire comparison of different data provisioning techniques:

The first comparison is with regards to data replicating properties:

Data replicating capabilities	SLT	SAP Data Services	Sybase Replication
Data movement	Real-time and scheduled replication	Scheduled replication	Real-time replication
Data Replication approach	Replication set up at the table level	Replication according to SAP Data Services configuration	Replication by Logical Unit of Work (LUW)
Presence of load balancing	Load balancing (parallelization)	Load balancing (parallelization)	No load balancing
Data transformation	Limited data transformations and filtering are possible	Complete ETL toolset for data transformations	No transformation of data
Supported tables	Transparent, pool, and cluster tables can be replicated	Transparent, pool, and cluster tables can be replicated	Transparent tables can be replicated. No support for pool and cluster tables, but consult OSS notes.
Support for compressed tables	Compressed tables are supported	Compressed tables are supported	Tables with compressed values are supported for DB2 Versions 9.1, 9.5, and 9.7. Row compressed tables only supported for DB2 Version 9.7.

The next comparison is with regards to the source system compatibility, as shown:

Source system compatibility	SLT	SAP Data Services	Sybase Replication
SAP Systems	SAP ERP systems from 4.6C, other ABAP based systems from Basis release 4.6C. For SAP systems, this is an RFC connection from SLT to the source system.	SAP ERP systems from 4.6C, other ABAP-based systems from Basis release 4.6C	SAP ERP 6.0
Non-SAP Systems	Any system on SAP supported database. For non-SAP systems, this is over a DB connection.	Any	Feasible in Sybase Replication Server, currently not in scope for SAP HANA though
Unicode	Unicode or non-Unicode source systems	Unicode or non-Unicode source systems	Unicode source systems only

The comparison with regards to the administration and configuration aspects is shown here:

Administration and Configuration aspects	SLT	SAP Data Services	Sybase Replication
Administration	Administration in SAP HANA Studio	Administration via regular SAP Data Services Management Console, or through SAP Solution Manager	Administration in SAP HANA Studio using the Load Controller component
Configuration	Some configuration in SLT server, especially with the first setup of new replication scenarios	Configuration in SAP Data Services	Configuration in Sybase Replication Server
Transformations	Transformations are configured and processed on the SLT server	Transformations are configured and processed in SAP Data Services	No transformations possible

See also

▸ Learn more about data provisioning in SAP HANA at `http://scn.sap.com/people/nagakishore.vankayala/blog/2011/12/09/data-provisioning-in-sap-hana`

▸ SAP Note: 1872673

Uploading data from flat files

Having learned about SAP HANA, its components, and its architecture, let's begin loading data into SAP HANA now. In this recipe, we will see how to load data from flat files.

Getting ready

To load data into SAP HANA from flat files, we will require the files in the form of a CSV or an Excel file (Office 1997 or above) saved in the client machine where we use SAP HANA Studio.

How to do it...

Let's load data into SAP HANA from an Excel sheet in three simple steps.

Step 1 – creating a table in the SAP HANA system

Initially, we create a table in the SAP HANA system. Then, we load the data to the newly created table. A table can be created either using SQL Console by writing a SQL code, or by using the graphical interface. We will see both the cases, as follows:

▸ **Using SQL Console**: From **Quick Launch**, select **SQL Console**. This will launch **SQL Console**. Write the following code and execute it to create a table. On successful execution, a message will appear in the status bar saying that the table creation is successful.

```
CREATE COLUMN TABLE "SYSTEM"."SAP_HANA_COOKBOOK"
(
NAME NVARCHAR (50),
ROLE NVARCHAR (50),
```

```
EMAIL_ID NVARCHAR (100)
);
```

This procedure is shown in the following screenshot:

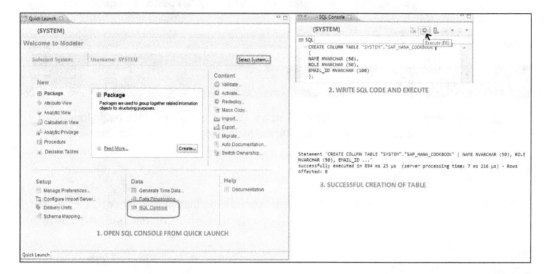

The preceding snippet of code will create a column table in the **SYSTEM** schema. We can also open SQL Console by selecting the appropriate schema instead of opening it from **Quick Launch**. In this case, the procedure will change as shown in the following screenshot, where we don't need to mention the schema name as **SYSTEM** while creating the table. This is because SQL Console will work on the schema that we select.

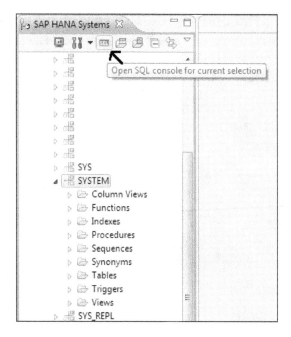

- ▶ **Using GUI**: Right-click on the **Tables** folder under the schema or on the schema name where we want to a create table, and select **New Table**. In our example, we will create a table in the **SYSTEM** schema, as shown in the following screenshot:

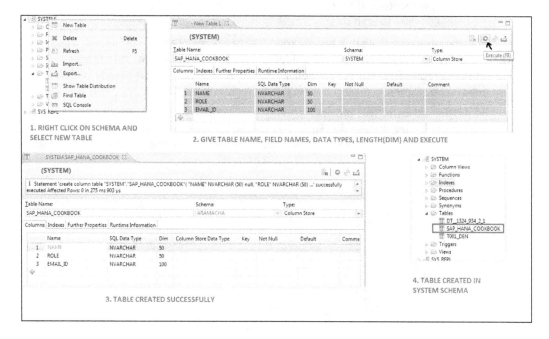

Step 2 – selecting the source file and target table in SAP HANA

From **Quick Launch**, select **Import**. Then select **Data from Local File** and click on **Next**, as shown in the following screenshot:

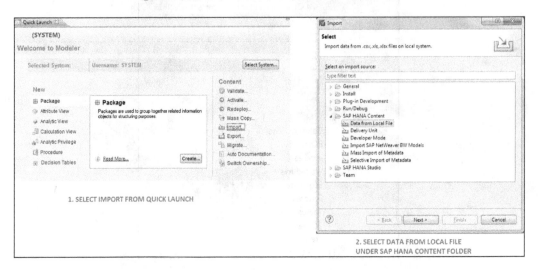

1. SELECT IMPORT FROM QUICK LAUNCH

2. SELECT DATA FROM LOCAL FILE
UNDER SAP HANA CONTENT FOLDER

Click on **Browse** and select the file. According to the data in the flat file, there are several options available to load data from the flat file to SAP HANA. They are discussed as follows:

- **Selecting worksheet**: If there are many worksheets in Excel, we can select which worksheet's data to load by selecting it from the drop-down menu.

- **Header rows**: If the file has header rows, we can eliminate them by selecting the checkbox. There may be more header rows in the file. Hence, the number of header rows field will be enabled, allowing us to enter the number of header rows to be ignored.

- **Importing all data**: This provides an option to either load all the data or selectively load data. By unchecking the **Import all data** checkbox, two more fields will be enabled to enter **Start Line** and **End Line**. Only the data in the range of these lines will be loaded.

▸ **Ignore leading and trailing white-space(s) in file**: This option eliminates all the leading/trailing whitespaces in the data, thereby kind of cleansing the data before loading.

These options are illustrated in the following screenshot:

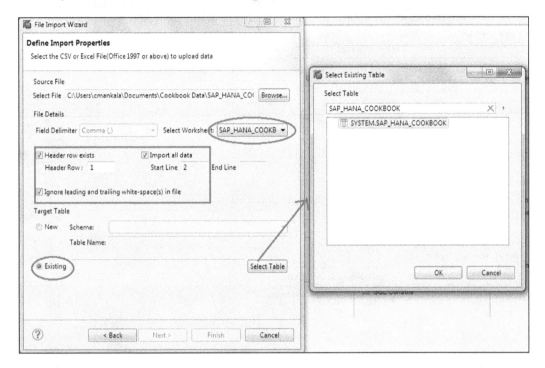

In the bottom portion of the **File Import Wizard** screen, select **Existing**, and then select the appropriate schema and table name.

Step 3 – field mapping and loading data

On selecting the file and target table, we are taken to the mapping area. Here we need to map the fields of file and table fields. We can manually map by selecting each field and dragging it to the other side. From the system side, we will have two options: **one-to-one** mapping and **Map By name**. Mapping can be done according to the fields. In this case, we go with **one-to-one** as the source and target fields are in the same sequence, as shown in the following screenshot:

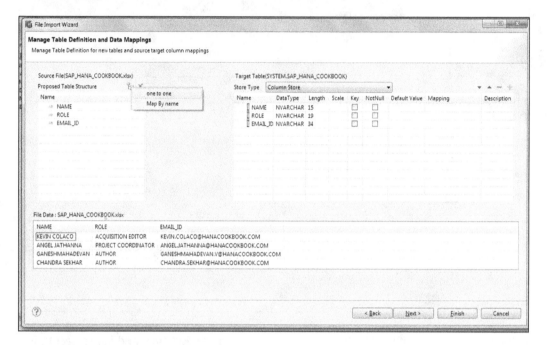

Once we select **one-to-one** mapping, we can see that the corresponding fields are mapped, as shown:

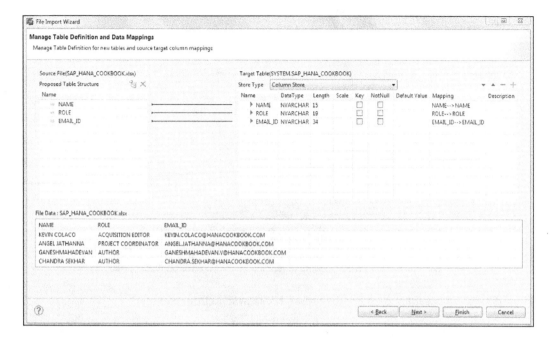

In the mapping screen, we can see sample data from the file. After the fields are mapped, click on **Next** to preview the data from both the file and the existing table. If data preview is not necessary and data has to be loaded on the go, select **Finish**. The confirmation is shown in the following screenshot:

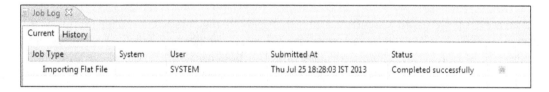

A job runs in the background to import the flat file and completes when the data is successfully imported. A data preview of the table will confirm the data is loaded, as shown in the following screenshot:

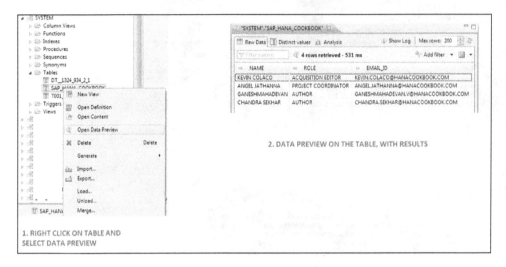

Thus, data is successfully loaded into the SAP HANA system from a flat file.

How it works...

Data can be loaded into SAP HANA tables directly from files using SAP HANA Studio. We don't need any data provisioning tool to load flat files' data. If we have multiple sheets in the Excel file, there is an option to select the required sheet and load the data. We can load data into a existing table or create a new table while loading the data itself.

If we are loading data in to an existing table in a schema, the data types and length must match in the files and tables; otherwise, we end up with errors while loading data. Whereas, when a table is created while loading data, data types and length will be given by the system according to the data in the file.

There's more...

We have seen how to load data in to an existing table. If a table is not available, the system will create a table in the required schema. After selecting the **Import** option from **Quick Launch**, we have to select **New** instead of selecting an existing radio button. In the next fields, **Schema** has to be selected and a new table name has to be given as **Table Name**. This will create a table in the schema selected, as shown in the following screenshot:

The system will propose new fields in the table, with the same names as that of the file, and the same data type as well. The next step remains the same, mapping and completing the data load, as shown in the following screenshot:

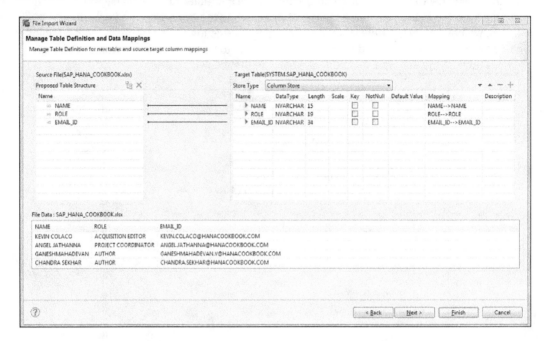

By default, a column table is created; we can see this in the top-right corner of the screen. If a row table is specifically required, **Store Type** should be changed to **Row Store**. On selecting this, the system will create a row table instead of the column table. The rest of the steps remain the same, mapping fields and loading the data, as shown in the following screenshot:

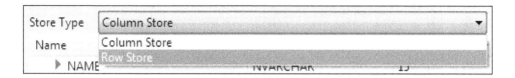

See also

▸   To learn more about loading data from a CSV file, visit:

    ❏   `http://www.saphana.com/docs/DOC-2362`

    ❏   `http://www.saphana.com/docs/DOC-2191`

Using SLT to load data into SAP HANA

SLT stands for SAP Landscape Transformation. We use this technique for real-time replication of the data from source systems—SAP/non-SAP. This method is primarily used for replication from SAP source systems. Apart from real-time replication, we can also use SLT for batch mode loads as well. When the required landscape contains both real-time and batch mode, SLT is the best. This recipe shows us how to load data into SAP HANA using SLT.

Getting ready

In order to load data using SLT, we must first ensure that real-time data loading is required. Also, the exact number of tables that have to be replicated should be known before going for SLT; replicating unnecessary tables involves a higher cost.

How to do it...

We will now see the steps to configure SLT and replicate data in SAP HANA.

SLT configuration – creating a connection

Connections can be created from transaction LTR in the SLT system. This t-code is a browser-based application. Hence, it will take us to the browser where we have to log in again with the SLT system credentials, as shown in the following screenshot:

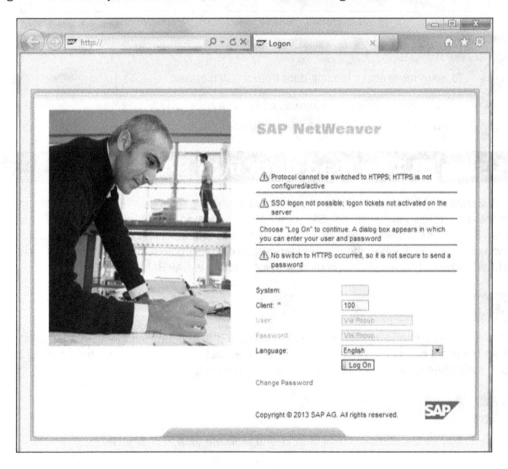

After logging in, the **Configuration and Monitoring Dashboard for HANA** panel will be opened, as shown in the following screenshot. Here, we will have options to create new connections and edit, delete, or check the status of the existing connections.

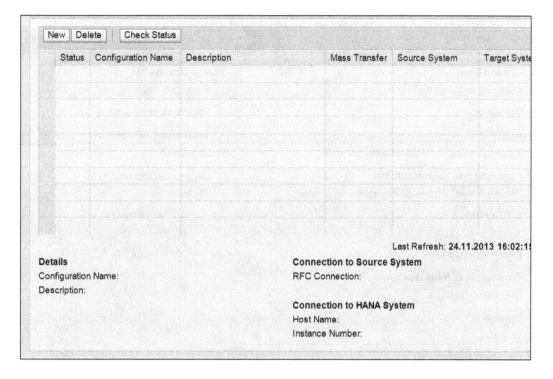

Now select **New** to create a connection. In the next step, the type of source system has to be selected, either **SAP System** or **Non-SAP System**. An RFC connection exists between the SAP source system and the SLT server, whereas a DB connection exists between the non-SAP and SLT server, as shown in the following screenshot:

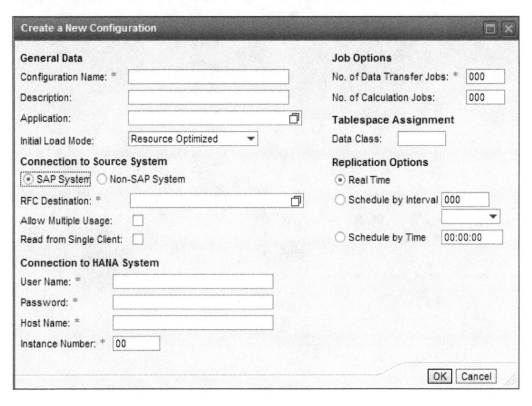

In the following screenshot, we can see that when we select **Non-SAP System** as the source, the drop-down menu changes, indicating the **Database System**.

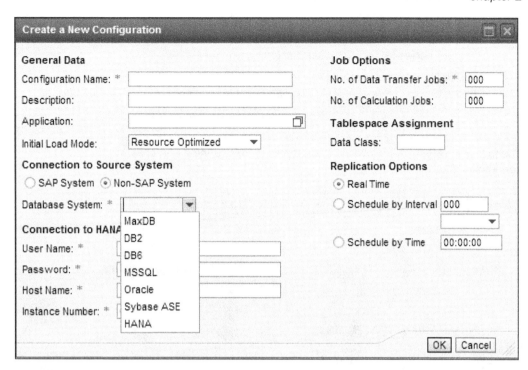

The mandatory parameters that have to be given to create a connection with the source system are as follows:

- **Configuration Name**: For each connection, whether SAP or non-SAP, a unique name has to be given.

- **RFC Destination**: For a SAP system: if the source is a SAP system, an RFC connection exists between the SLT server and SAP source. From the list of available RFC connections, one connection has to be selected. These RFC connections have to be created in t-code SM59 in the same way as you created connections between SAP systems.

- **Database System**: For a non-SAP system, a database connection will be created between the source and the SLT server. Different databases that are supported are shown in the preceding screenshot.

- ▶ **Connection to HANA System**: SAP HANA details—**Host Name**, **Instance Number**, **User Name**, and **Password** are to be entered. These details are required to connect the SLT server to the target SAP HANA system.

- ▶ **No. of Data Transfer Jobs**: Data transfer jobs are responsible for replicating data to the SAP HANA system. This can be set depending on the available background jobs in the SLT server.

Once a connection is created, we can see all the details and edit the parameters. The following screenshot shows us the number of jobs running and their connection status:

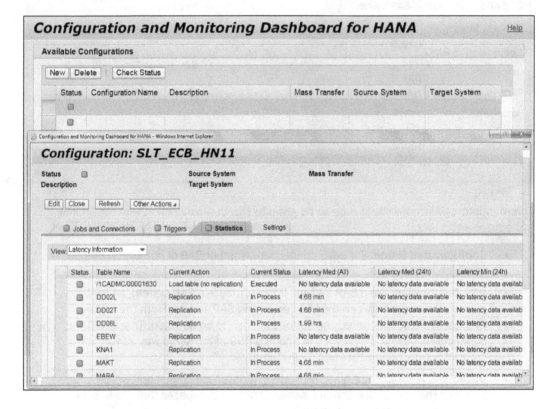

These parameters can be changed; we can edit a number of jobs and other options as shown in the following screenshot:

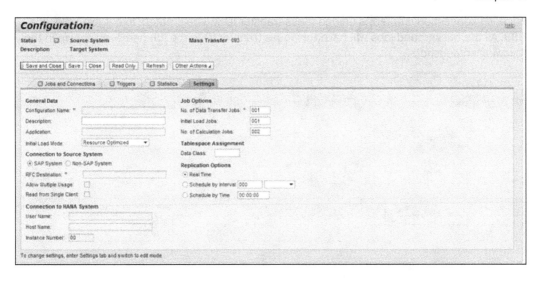

Each connection will have a unique **Mass Transfer** ID. In the screenshot, the **Mass Transfer** ID is **093**.

For each connection, jobs will be scheduled in the SLT server. This can be monitored from t-code SM37. Different jobs will be scheduled in the background up on creating a connection. They are given as follows:

- `IUUC_MONITOR_<mass_transfer_id>`: This job monitors the status of the system connection. This is the first job that will be created up on creating the connection. This job recreates the other jobs.

- `IUUC_REPLIC_CNTR_xxx_yyyy`: This is a replication control job (where `xxx` and `yyyy` are digits). Whenever there is a change in logging tables, this job runs and picks up all the data and writes to the SAP HANA system. These jobs will be always in a released state, and they start and complete in seconds. If these jobs run for a long time, that is, for minutes, it indicates that something is wrong or there is a huge amount of data to be transferred to SAP HANA.

- `DTL_MT_DATA_LOAD_xxx_yy`: This is a data load job. This job should always be in an active state for data loading to happen. When there are data loading issues, cancelling these jobs will resolve the issues. These jobs will be recreated automatically from `IUUC_MONITOR_<mass_transfer_id>`.

For each connection created, a unique mass transfer ID will be created. In our example, it is **093**. All the background jobs will have this mass transfer ID in the job name, as shown in the following screenshot:

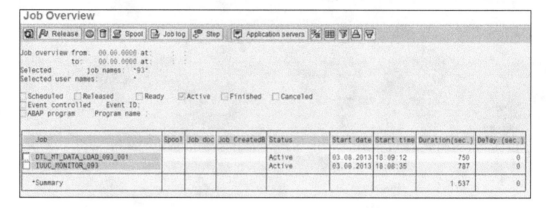

These are the steps to create a connection with the source system and monitor the status. Now let's see how to load data into SAP HANA using SAP HANA Studio.

From **Quick Launch** in SAP HANA Studio, select **Data Provisioning**. Now we will see the available connections in **Select Source System** and the corresponding schema in the **Target Schema Configured** list, as shown in the following screenshot. From the available connections, select a connection where data has to be loaded into SAP HANA.

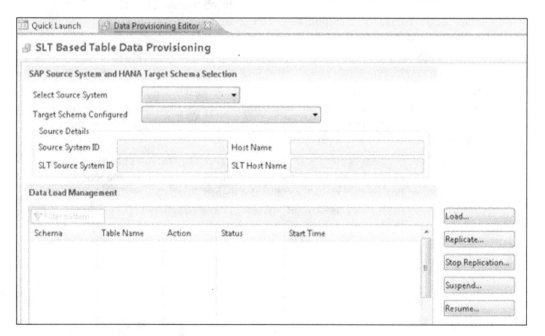

Here we have five options—**Load...**, **Replicate...**, **Stop Replication...**, **Suspend...**, and **Resume....** Each action has its own prominence. This is as explained as follows:

▶ **Load**: This will dump all the data from the source to SAP HANA. It is a single-time load. Furthermore, if there are any changes or if new data is created in the source system, the changes will not be replicated to SAP HANA. All the data present in the source system table at the time of starting this activity will be loaded into SAP HANA. Triggers and logging tables are not created when we use the **Load** option. Hence, when a **Load** option is used, it is recommended to drop all the data in the table and then go with **Load**. If we load data without dropping it, data will be duplicated.

Click on **Load** and search for the table that has to be loaded into SAP HANA. We can select multiple tables at a time and start loading them, as shown in the following screenshot:

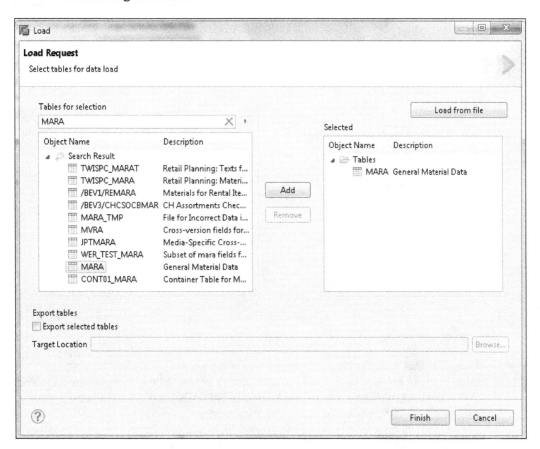

▶ **Replicate**: This is similar to the **Load** action, except that **Replicate** creates triggers and logging tables in the source system. Hence, when there is new data or a change in data, this will be captured in logging tables and replicated to the target SAP HANA table. When we replicate a table, the status of the selected table will be **In Process**. This means replication is in process and whenever there is new or altered data, this will be loaded to SAP HANA.

▶ **Stop Replication**: This action stops the replication process. This will delete the triggers and logging tables for the selected table. Hence, no more altered or new data will be replicated to SAP HANA. When we stop replication, we have to drop the table content before we select **Replicate** again, as shown in the following screenshot:

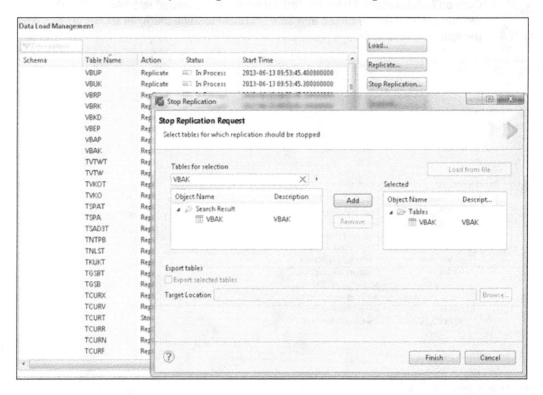

▶ **Suspend**: This will stop the replicating process temporarily. Triggers and logging tables will not be deleted, but they just become inactive. All the changes are captured in the logging tables and this can be loaded to SAP HANA using the **Resume** option, without losing data and compromising data integrity. It is recommended not to suspend loads for a long time, as the size of the logging tables in the source system will increase, which becomes a burden after resuming the loads.

▶ **Resume**: This option will resume data loading from the last suspended state. All the changes captured in the logging tables since the last suspend action will be loaded to SAP HANA upon resuming.

How it works...

SLT can be used for data replication from a SAP or non-SAP source system. The installation of SLT Replication Server depends on the type of source system that we connect with. If the source system is SAP, SLT Replication Server can be installed on a separate SAP system or in the existing SAP system itself, depending on the technical constraints. If the source system is a non-SAP system, SAP Replication Server has to be installed on a separate system. However, it is best to install SLT on a separate machine, as maintenance activities such as upgrades and applying patches will be easier. This avoids impact on the SAP source system when there are software changes in the SLT system.

For data replication, settings have to be maintained. This involves creating connections between the source and target systems. All these configurations have to be made in SLT Replication Server. The configuration details include the source system, target system, and type of connection. We can replicate data from one source to one target system (1:1), for example, the SAP HANA system, from multiple sources to a single target system (N:1), or from one source system to multiple target systems (1:N). Furthermore, we can also specify the nature of the load: either real-time, or scheduled by time or interval.

SLT is a trigger-based approach to loading data, where data is replicated from the application tables of the source system. After the required configurations are done, we can select the tables from SAP HANA Studio for replication. All the data from the table can be loaded, or selective loading is possible by creating transformation rules and filtering data.

The following diagram shows us how the architecture will look if SLT is configured on the same server on which SAP ECC is installed.

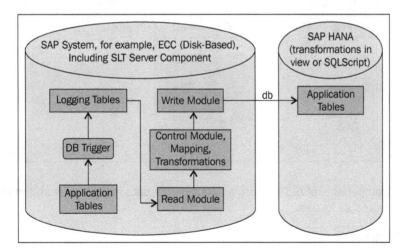

As explained earlier, installing SLT on a separate server is always recommended as maintenance becomes easy. The following diagram shows us the architecture if SLT is installed on a separate server, connecting SAP ECC and SAP HANA:

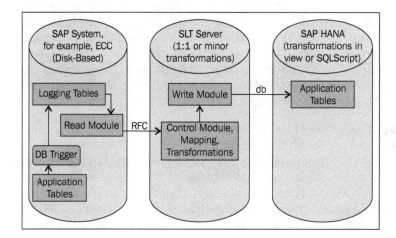

Having seen the architecture of the SLT configuration with SAP ECC as the source system, the following diagram explains the architecture when the source system is a non-SAP system:

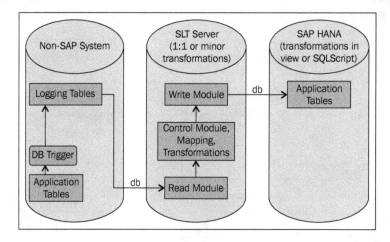

The different components of SLT that are responsible for data replication from the source to the target are given as follows:

- Logging tables
- Read module
- Control module
- Write module

Logging tables

When an application table is replicated, logging tables and database triggers are automatically created on the source system side. After the table is replicated for the first time, DB triggers read any change in these application tables and immediately store the changes in the logging tables. After data is written to the target system, the data in the logging tables is cleared.

Read module

Read modules take data from the logging tables and pass the data as requested by the control module. The placement of read modules depends on the source system. If the source system is SAP, then read modules will be installed on the SAP system itself. If the source system is a non-SAP system, read modules will be installed on the SLT server. Read modules also take care of the declustering of the table classes into a transparent format.

Control module

The control modules that reside on the SLT Replication Server instance manage the replication process and initiate data replication through the read modules in the source system to the SAP HANA system. Control modules ensure mapping between the SAP HANA database structure and the structure of the source system. Field conversion or migration abilities are only provided by the control modules, for example, the requirement may be to have data fields as strings. This can be achieved with the help of control modules. The data replication process is managed by these modules. The data load frequency can be set, whether it has to be a real-time load or a periodic load that is based on a time interval. All these features are included in these modules. After reading data from the read module, the control module takes care of all the intermediate activities, such as field conversions and load frequency, and then the data is passed to the write module. Then, the the control module activates the triggers of the write module.

Write module

The main purpose of a write module is to write data to the SAP HANA system through a DB connection. This module also offers flexibility to switch from single operation (that is, insert or update or delete) to the array operations.

There's more...

Apart from replicating all the data, we can also replicate data by maintaining additional settings. This can be done in the t-code `IUUC_REPL_CONTENT` as illustrated in the following screenshot:

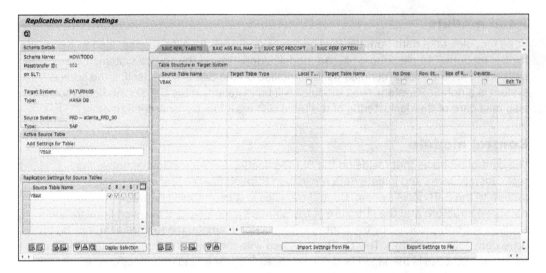

Settings have to be maintained for individual tables. Input the table name on the left-hand side of the screen and maintain the settings in the right-hand section.

See also

- ► SLT Replication Server Cockpit: Transaction code `IUUC_SYNC_MON`
- ► You can learn more about real-time replication from the SAP system to HANA using SLT at `http://sapanalyticsguru.com/index.php/sap-hana/33-realtime-replication-from-sap-system-to-hana-using-slt`

- ▸ *Trigger-Based Data Replication Using SAP Landscape Transformation Replication Server* at `http://help.sap.com/hana/SAP_HANA_Installation_Guide_Trigger_Based_Replication_SLT_en.pdf`

- ▸ You can find the list of all available SAP notes at `http://scn.sap.com/community/replication-server/blog/2013/02/27/list-of-all-slt-notes`

Using SAP Data Services as an ETL tool to load data into SAP HANA

We use SAP Data Services to load data into SAP HANA when there are high transformations to be applied before loading. When the scheduled data load is enough, real-time data loading is not required. We can also make use of DS with a real-time mechanism when non-SAP sources are included. In this recipe, we will see the steps to load data using SAP DS to SAP HANA.

Getting ready

To load data using SAP DS, we need a minimum of SAP DS Version 4.0 or higher and SAP HANA installed.

How to do it...

Of the four ways mentioned to create tables, we have already seen the first two ways using SAP HANA Studio, that is, GUI and SQL Console in the *Uploading data from flat files* recipe.

Now we will see how to create tables using the import of metadata option from SAP DS.

Creating table in SAP HANA using the import of metadata option

This can be done in four simple steps.

Step 1 – Creating a datastore for the source system in SAP Data Services

Follow these steps:

1. Navigate to the **Datastores** section in SAP DS **Designer** and right-click in **Local Object Library**—an empty area. Select **New** from the context menu, as shown in the following screenshot:

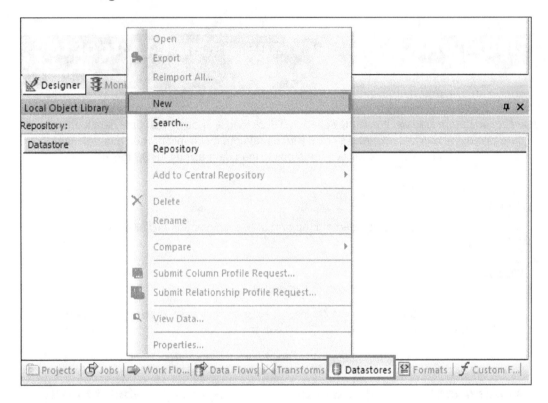

2. Give the name of the **Datastore** to be created, **Datastore type**, and other details. If we are creating the datastore as a SAP system as the source, we have to mention the **Database server name** and login credentials of the SAP system, as shown in the following screenshot:

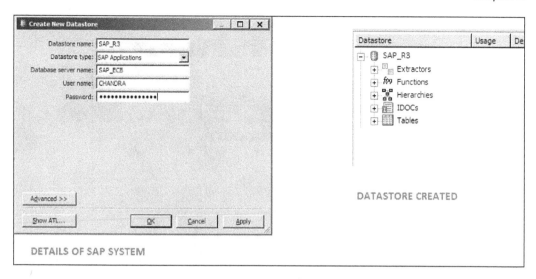

DATASTORE CREATED

DETAILS OF SAP SYSTEM

If we are connecting to external databases such as Oracle and MS SQL, we need to input **Database version**, **Database server name**, and the login credentials of the database, as shown in the following screenshot:

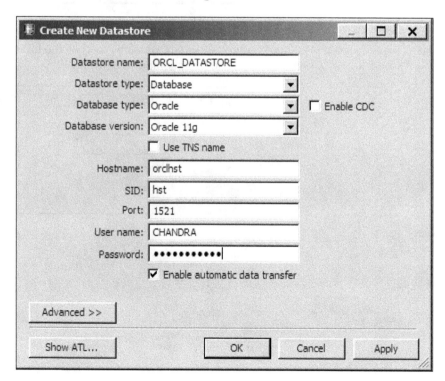

The following screenshot shows the various database types:

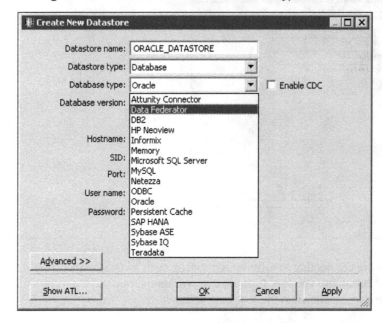

Step 2 – Importing tables in SAP DS for the datastore created

We will import the required tables from the source system. We can import all the tables or import the individual tables by name, as shown in the following screenshot:

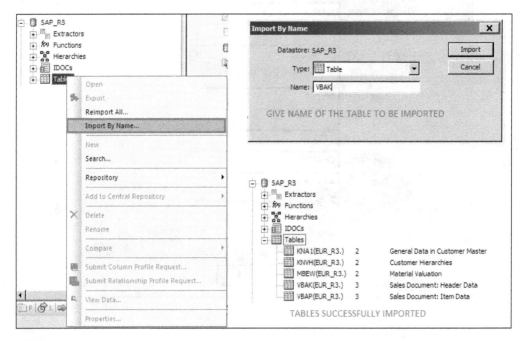

Step 3 – Configuring Import Server from the Quick Launch screen of SAP HANA Studio

Here, details about SAP DS have to be given—DS **Server Address**, **Repository Name**, **ODBC Data Source**, and **Default Port** number, as shown in the following screenshot:

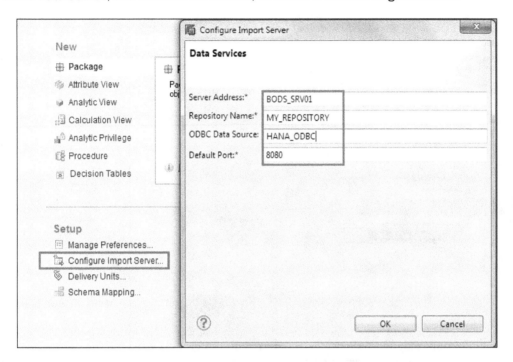

Step 4 – Importing metadata from SAP HANA Studio

The table that is imported into SAP DS has to be imported into SAP HANA. From the **Quick Launch** screen, select **Import** followed by **Selective Import of Metadata** under the **SAP HANA Content** folder, as shown in the following screenshot:

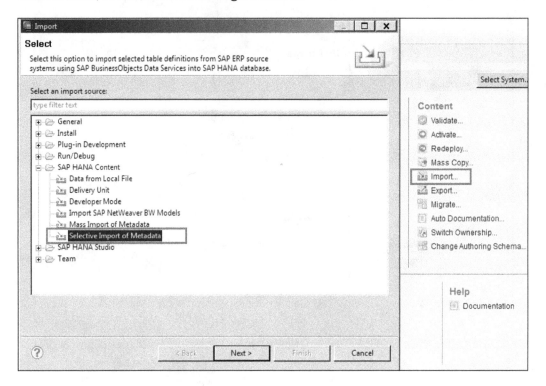

In the next screen, we will see the list of available connections. Select a source connection from the drop-down list, as shown in the following screenshot:

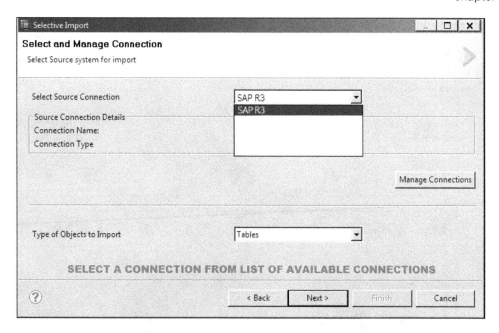

Search for the table to be imported. Select the required table and add it to the target side. Select the target schema against the **Select Schema** dropdown, as shown in the following screenshot:

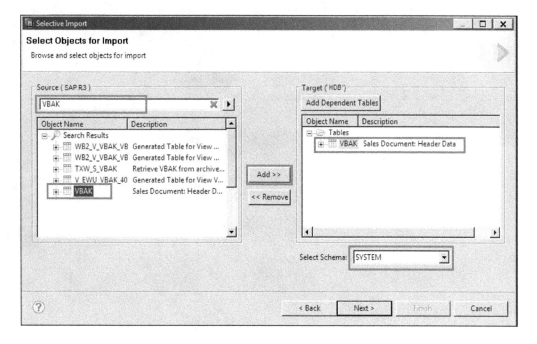

In the next screen, select the table and click on **Validate**. Once validation is successful, we can see a green tick mark under the **Status** tab, as shown in the following screenshot:

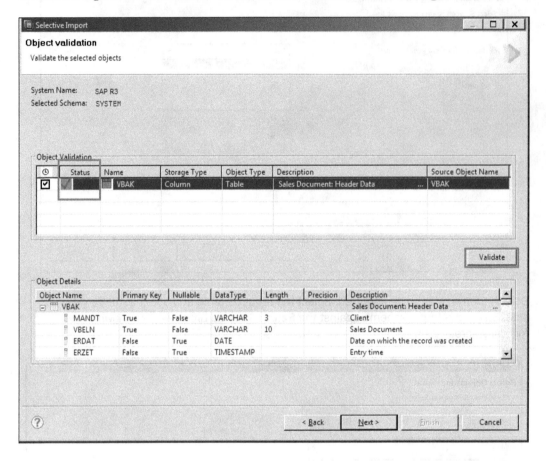

Go to the next screen and click on **Finish** to import the metadata of the table into SAP HANA. This will create a table in the specified schema.

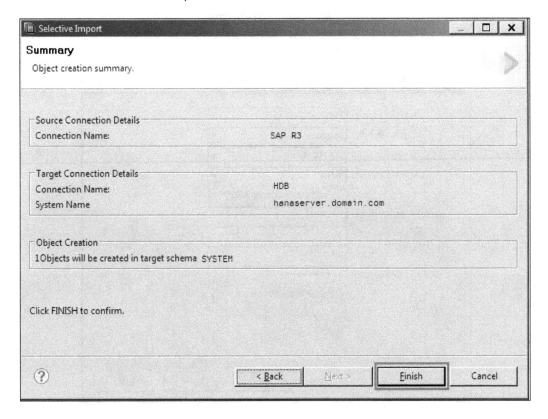

Creating a datastore for a target system – SAP HANA in SAP Data Services

Also create a datastore for the SAP HANA system, as discussed previously. Details such as **Database version**, **Datastore name**, and login credentials of SAP HANA system are required, as shown in the following screenshot:

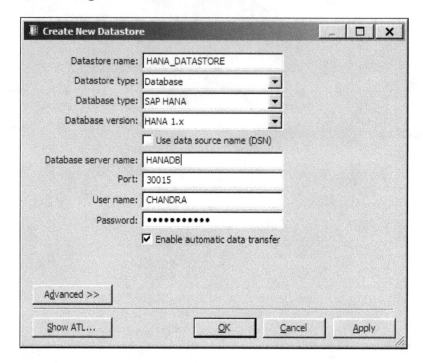

Creating a project

A project can hold any number of jobs, data flows, and workflows. Projects group and organize related objects. We can place related objects into one project.

To create a project, select **Create Project** from the start page or by navigating to **Project | New | Project**, and name the project, as shown in the following screenshot:

Creating a job

A job is a reusable object, which is at the second level in the project hierarchy. It contains workflows and data flows. We can execute jobs manually or they can be scheduled.

To add a new job, right-click in the project area, select the **New Batch Job**, and name the job as shown in the following screenshot:

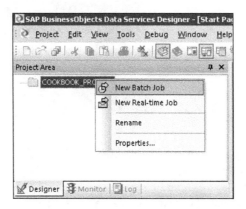

Creating a workflow

A workflow is a reusable object. It executes only within a job. Workflows are optional. Workflows can be used to do the following:

- ▶ Call data flows
- ▶ Call another workflow
- ▶ Define the order of steps that will be executed in the job
- ▶ Pass parameters to and from the data flows
- ▶ Define conditions for implementing sections of the project
- ▶ Identify and handle errors that occur during the execution

To create a workflow, select the icon from the tool palette. Name the new workflow. Renaming can be done in the manner similar to renaming the job. Click on the workflow to open it in the workspace. Now we are working in the workflow, as shown in the following screenshot:

Creating a data flow

A data flow is a reusable object. It is always contained in a workflow or a job, hence it gets the call from the same. A data flow defines the flow of data from the source to target. It is used to do the following:

- ▶ Identify the source data that has to be read
- ▶ Define the transformations that are to be performed on the data
- ▶ Identify the target table to which data has to be loaded

To create a data flow, select the  icon from the tools palette. Name the new data flow. Renaming can be done in a manner similar to renaming the job. Click on the data flow to open it in the workspace. Now we are currently working in the data flow, as shown in the following screenshot:

Designing the data flow

Include the imported tables from the source and target datastores in the data flow. According to the complexity of the job design, data cleansing and query transformations have to be included. In this example, we add a simple query transformation, and map fields between the source and target tables, as shown in the following screenshot:

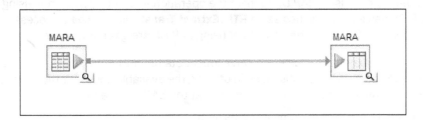

Validating the data flow and saving the project

After the data flow is designed with all the required objects, it has to be validated for errors. The validation menu offers design-time validation options such as syntax error, and non-runtime errors. Runtime validation happens during the job execution. A pop-up comes up with the result if there are any errors, as shown in the following screenshot:

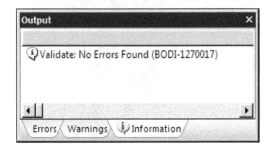

After validation is successful, the project has to be saved so that the jobs designed under that project are ready to be executed.

Executing the job

The job created with the data flow and workflow has to be executed to start the actual process and load data into SAP HANA. We can configure the settings such as selecting a job server before running the job. On starting the job, we can monitor the job log and check whether it completes successfully or not.

How it works...

SAP Data Services is intended primarily for batch mode processing. Real-time loading is also possible, but its capabilities are very low compared to SLT. We cannot load a huge volume of data in real time by using SAP DS to meet the operational reporting scenarios using SAP HANA. SAP DS has got capabilities as an **ETL** (**Extract Transform** and **Load**) process. It has the functionalities of ETL and the benefits of using SAP DS are given as follows:

> ▸ For SAP systems as source, we can extract data not only from tables, but also from existing data sources. This helps in utilizing the available codes for the extractors, thereby minimizing the modeling activity at the SAP HANA end.

> ▸ Metadata can also be transferred using SAP DS.

> ▸ Delta capabilities are also available in SAP DS, which can be leveraged.

Before starting to load data from SAP DS to SAP HANA, we need the schema and tables available in the SAP HANA system. Creating tables can be done in several ways:

- From SAP HANA Studio, by using GUI

- From SAP HANA Studio, by using SQL Console

- From SAP HANA Studio, by using mass import of metadata—only for SAP source systems

- From SAP DS, by executing a job

The tables created by the execution of SAP DS will not allow us to change the table definition before loading the data. The job will create the table and load data as a part of the same job immediately. After the data is loaded, we cannot alter the field definitions, that is, changing the field type or length is not possible. Hence, it is recommended to create the required tables before starting the data loads.

There's more...

In the previous section, we have seen that tables are created beforehand in SAP HANA. The tables can also be created during the execution of a DS job. For this, instead of taking imported table from the SAP HANA datastore, we can include a template table as a target in the data flow. By doing this, DS will create a table in the target schema, similar to the source table, with all the field definitions and types. Then the data will be loaded to the created table immediately. We cannot modify this table definition. To do this, data has to be deleted and then the table definition has to be changed.

See also

- *SAP Data Services 4.2 (14.2.0)* at `http://help.sap.com/businessobject/product_guides/sbods42/en/ds_42_install_win_en.pdf`

- Learn more about loading data from source to HANA using BODS at `http://sapanalyticsguru.com/index.php/sap-bods/30-loading-data-from-source-to-hana-using-bods`

- Learn more about data provisioning using BI 4.0 Data Services at `http://scn.sap.com/docs/DOC-26311`

- Learn more about working with data using SAP Data Services at `http://www.saphana.com/community/implement/hana-academy#working-with-data-sap-data-services`

Loading data into SAP HANA using DXC

This recipe explains how to load data into SAP HANA by using **Direct Extractor Connection (DXC)**.

Getting ready

The data provisioning techniques we have come across so far require separate installation of the software components. Using DXC, we can load data into SAP HANA from the SAP source systems. Also, we can use all the standard data sources that come as a part of SAP Business Content, which were originally developed with the use of SAP **Business Information Warehouse (BW)**. We go for DXC mostly in the case of BW on HANA. SAP BW will use all the data sources delivered and their related data objects, such as **DataStore Object (DSO)** and cubes, for deployment. SAP standard data sources are built on several base application tables. Re-implementing these in SAP HANA by replicating individual tables involves high costs and a lot of work. DXC allows us to use all the standard data sources, and data can be loaded to SAP HANA in the same way as we load data into SAP BW. The embedded SAP BW instance in the SAP source system will become less unusable for reporting. Keeping future scope in perspective, we may have more work if more operational reporting is moved on to SAP HANA, as data foundation levels will be missing. As DXC uses SAP standard Business Content DataSources, we can leverage all the delta capabilities of the extractors while loading data to SAP HANA. Let's get to know more about DXC.

How to do it...

First of all, we need to configure DXC and then start loading data to SAP HANA.

Configuring DXC

The steps involved in setting up DXC are as follows:

1. Enable SAP HANA XS and SAP Web Dispatcher Services/ICM in SAP HANA, as follows:

    □   SAP HANA XS Engine is in-built in SAP HANA. This engine is capable of processing the incoming HTTP requests, even multi-packet requests. The HTTP requests are parsed by XS Engine. Without this engine, HTTP requests cannot be parsed. SAP Web Dispatcher Services and ICM are responsible for communication between the SAP system and the outside world through HTTP requests.

    □   These services must be enabled, and they should be up and running in order to connect SAP HANA with the DXC system. From an administration perspective, these services can be enabled and it can be ensured that these are up and running. In the Administration perspective, under the `daemon.ini` section, check for `sapwebdisp` and `xsengine`. For both of these, the value should be `1`, with a green light against it.

2. Set up SAP HANA Direct Extractor Connection, as follows:

   ❑ The delivery unit has to be imported to start using DXC. The delivery unit comprises built-in models for the SAP HANA system. DXC will be provided by SAP, which can be downloaded from SAP Marketplace. After importing the delivery unit, ensure that all the objects are active.

   ❑ Configuration settings for DXC to use `xsengine` have to be maintained. In the following path, a value of `libxsdxclibxsdxc` has to be set for `application_list`:

   Administration Console | Configuration | xsengine.ini | application_ container | application_list

3. Create a DXC user in SAP HANA

   ❑ A user has to be created, which will be used by DXC to log in to SAP HANA and transfer data. In the navigation pane, create a user from the security folder. Assign the roles `PUBLIC` and `MONITORING` to the user created.

4. Create a DXC schema in SAP HANA:

   ❑ Create a new schema to hold all the data of DXC. This schema must be owned by the DXC user created in the previous step.

5. Create a HTTP connection to the SAP HANA system:

   ❑ Log in to the SAP Business Suite system and create a HTTP connection for a target SAP HANA system. This can be done in t-code SM59.

6. Configure DXC HTTP Interface Destination:

   ❑ In SAP Business Suite system, call t-code SA38 and execute the `SAP_RSADMIN_MAINTAIN` program. For the `PSA_TO_HDB_DESTINATION` object, enter the SAP HANA HTTP destination and execute. This will create an entry in the `RSADMIN` table.

7. Choose the system-wide setting for DataSources.

   ❑ We have to configure settings to determine which BW system has to be used for DXC: embedded BW or remote login.

8. Designate the schema in SAP HANA to store **In-Memory DataStore Object** (**IMDSO**).

   ❑ For each DataSource, one IMDSO will be generated. The schema name that these objects have to be stored under has to be designated. The schema created in step 4 has to be used for this purpose.

Loading data to SAP HANA

After configuring DXC with source and SAP HANA, we can load data into SAP HANA.
Follow these steps:

- ▸ **Installing Business Content**: Business Content has to be installed. This Business Content will contain the data sources.

- ▸ **Replicating data sources**: Replicate the required data sources that created data sources on the embedded BW system. Now these data sources can be activated.

- ▸ **Checking IMDSOs in SAP HANA**: When data sources are activated, IMDSOs for each data source are created in the SAP HANA system. Once activation of data sources is done, it should be ensured that all the IMDSOs are properly created; especially with respect to the primary key definition under the DXC schema that was created earlier.

- ▸ **Creating and executing InfoPackages/process chains**: Loads are executed from an embedded (or side-by-side) BW system. For this, all the required objects, such as InfoPackages and process chains, are created. These are executed to load data.
  Now the data will be directly loaded to SAP HANA IMDSO using the HTTP connection.

How it works...

DXC is not only a data provisioning technique to load data to SAP HANA, but it also helps to create IMDSOs in the SAP HANA system to hold the data that DXC sends. A HTTP connection exists between DXC and SAP HANA, as shown in the following diagram:

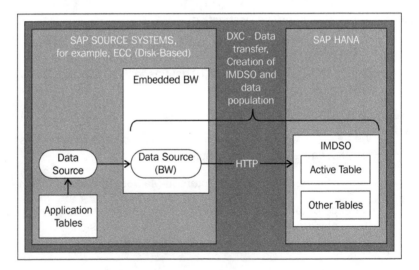

DXC can be deployed in three different ways, as follows:

- ▶ With a SAP source system on SAP NetWeaver Version 7.0 or higher, using the embedded SAP NetWeaver BW system
- ▶ With a SAP source system on a version below SAP NetWeaver 7.0, using a side-by-side SAP NetWeaver BW system
- ▶ With a SAP HANA system for the BW system

Let's briefly walk through each deployment option.

An SAP source system on SAP NetWeaver Version 7.0 or higher, using the embedded SAP NetWeaver BW system

This is the default configuration of DXC. This uses the embedded NetWeaver BW system's functionalities to load data from the source system to SAP HANA directly. No data is stored in this embedded BW system, but only the functionalities such as InfoPackages and process chains will be used to load data from the data sources that work with DXC.

An SAP source system on a version below SAP NetWeaver 7.0, using a side-by-side SAP NetWeaver BW system

We can still use DXC even though the SAP source system is on a release prior to SAP NetWeaver 7.0. But to do so, we need a separate installation of the SAP NetWeaver BW system. The purpose of this BW system remains same as that of an embedded BW system. We cannot use this for storing data and reporting purposes (the design of DSO and InfoCubes is not allowed). The sole purpose of this BW system will be to transfer data to SAP HANA. This configuration is known as a "side-by-side" or "Sidecar" implementation of SAP NetWeaver BW.

Data flow from DXC to SAP HANA takes place as shown here:

- ▶ Using existing data sources, data is extracted and the user exits are called
- ▶ Data from a data source is transferred to the BW system (embedded or side-by-side or SAP HANA for BW system)
- ▶ Local data source replicas in BW receive the data and transfer it to SAP HANA IMDSO using the HTTP connection
- ▶ The data received by IMDSO will be initially stored in the activation queue
- ▶ Once activation is completed, the data will be available in an active table of IMDSO, ready for use by the data models

Before implementing DXC, there are a few points to be considered. These are explained as follows:

- **Layering/Data transformations**: In any technique of implementing DXC, we load the data directly to SAP HANA IMDSOs. We don't use BW to stage or layer of the data. Hence, it is not possible to transform the data according to the business requirements after loading, for example, in transfer rules or transformations. Everything should be done at the source system itself before loading. The only change in this case is the use of user exits.

- **Data source availability**: Data source availability depends on the type of DXC deployment.

  In the case of an embedded or side-by-side setup of DXC, the data source can be used to load data to another installation of the BW system that runs out of a different database. The same data source cannot be used by the embedded BW system to populate data. This is because the data source will be flagged as a configuration for use with DXC.

  In the case of SAP HANA for a BW deployment, the data sources used in DXC cannot be used to load BW data flows.

- **Primary keys in IMDSO**: The IMDSO object in BW is just a table; it must have a primary key. Hence, it must be ensured that the data source provides a primary key definition and also, data sources must be well-suited for the overwrite mechanism of DSO.

There's more...

Let's have a look at an interesting feature called the "Sidecar" approach.

The Sidecar approach

The Sidecar approach comes in to the picture when DXC has to be implemented with an older SAP Business Suite system, which is not based on SAP NetWeaver 7.0 or higher (for example, 4.6C). In other cases, the embedded BW is already in use, so we cannot use it for DXC. Even though an embedded BW system on a SAP Business Suite system is primarily used for scheduling and monitoring extraction jobs in the DXC scenario, we might choose to avoid its use. When these conditions exist, we can implement DXC with the Sidecar approach.

With the Sidecar approach, instead of using an embedded BW system inside the SAP Business Suite system, we use a separate connected BW system as an intermediary system for scheduling and managing the extraction job in the connected SAP Business Suite system. This system sends the extracted data directly to SAP HANA. The data extracted is not loaded into the connected SAP BW system; instead, the data flow is redirected to the SAP HANA system.

See also

▸ SAP Note 1677278 and SAP Note 1701750 for more information on data source primary key constraints

▸ Learn more about the usage of DXC at `http://www.saphana.com/docs/DOC-2420`

Loading data using SAP Sybase Replication Server

This recipe deals with loading data into SAP HANA using Sybase Replication Server.

Getting ready

We use different data provisioning techniques to load data into SAP HANA based on several factors. We use Sybase Replication majorly when real-time data replication is required from non-SAP systems. In the latest release of SAP Sybase Replication Server Version 15.7.1 SP100, available since June 2013, data replication to SAP HANA is also supported. As of now, Sybase has been certified only with non-SAP applications. Certification and support for SAP applications is expected in the near future, with the next release of SAP Sybase Replication Server.

How to do it...

A configuration has to be set up prior to starting the replication of data into SAP HANA. The steps involved in configuring the setup differ for different databases. These include system requirements, installation of required drivers, and so on. In this recipe, we will see the steps involved in the setup of Oracle to SAP HANA Replication.

Oracle to SAP HANA Replication setup

In this recipe, we will see the steps involved in the setup of Oracle to SAP HANA Replication. The prerequisites and the steps involved in configuration are explained here. Let's have a look at the various aspects.

Prerequisites

Here's a list of prerequisites for the setup:

- A minimum of Oracle 10g is required. Oracle 10g or 11g Enterprise Edition is installed and configured as a primary database for Replication Server. Replication Agent replicates transactions from the configured database.

- SAP HANA should be installed and configured as the target database. The installed SAP HANA system is connected to Replication Server using **ExpressConnect for HANA (ECH)**.

- Oracle JDBC Thin drivers are to be installed. This depends on the release of Oracle installed as the primary database:

  - If Oracle 10g or 11g release 1 is installed as the primary database, then Oracle JDBC Thin driver is required for Oracle 10g or 11g and JDK 1.4 and 1.5

  - If Oracle 10g or 11g release 2 is installed as the primary database, then Oracle JDBC Thin driver 11.2 is required for JDK 1.6

- All hosts must have TCP/IP connectivity.

- The required operating system patches for Java have to be installed.

- Replication Agent must have access to the Oracle online and archived redo logs.

Configuring Replication Server to SAP HANA

The following steps need to be taken:

1. If we are connected to the SAP HANA database with a standard connection (and are not using SAP Secure User Store), an entry to your Replication Server interfaces file has to be added, identifying the replicate SAP HANA database. Then stop and start Replication Server, as shown:

   ```
   [dataservername]
   master tcp ether hostname port
   query tcp ether hostname port
   ```

   Here, `hostname` and `port` are the SAP HANA database's host and port. `dataservername` is a label used to identify the host and port number.

2. If we are using SAP Secure User Store, a user store has to be created with encrypted credentials:

   ```
   hdbuserstore set
   rdsrdsmyhost:xxxxxmy_securestore_userusermy_securestore_
   pwd
   ```

Here,

- ❏ `rds`: This is the key for the secure store entry
- ❏ `myhost:xxxxx`: This is the connection environment host name and port number
- ❏ `my_securestore_user` and `my_securestore_pwd`: These are the SAP Secure User Store credentials

3. On the SAP HANA database, create a maintenance user by following these steps:

   1. Create a user ID with a temporary password:

      ```
      CREATE USER m_user PASSWORD m_pwd_temp
      ```

   2. Update the temporary password after logging in to this system with the old password:

      ```
      ALTER USER m_user PASSWORD m_pwd_new
      ```

   3. Test the new password by logging out and then logging in again.

   4. Log into the SAP HANA database:

      ```
      ./hdbsql -u user -p password -iiid
      ```

      Here, `user` is the SAP HANA database user, `password` is the user password, and `id` is the instance number.

   5. On the SAP HANA database, grant the following authorities to the maintenance user, as shown:

      ```
      GRANT CREATE ANY, DELETE, DROP, EXECUTE, INDEX, SELECT,
      UPDATE ON SCHEMA my_schema TO m_user
      ```

      Here, `my_schema` is the SAP HANA database schema, and `m_user` is the maintenance user that has been just created.

   6. Log into Replication Server, as shown here:

      ```
      isql –Usa –Psa_pass –SSAMPLE_RS
      ```

      If a sample Replication Server instance has not been set up, the Replication Server instance name has to be given in place of `SAMPLE_RS`.

   7. Create a connection to the replicate SAP HANA database instance using ExpressConnect for HANA DB.

8. Use `admin show_connections, 'replicate'` to see the replicated connection that has been created:

For a standard connection:

```
create connection to rds.rdb
using profile rs_oracle_to_hanadb;ech
set username m_user
set password m_pwd
go
```

For SAP Secure User Store:

```
create connection to rds.rdb
using profile rs_oracle_to_hanadb;ech
set username auser
set password apwd
setsetdsi_connector_sec_mech to "hdbuserstore"
go
```

Here,

- ❑ `rds`: This is the replicated SAP HANA database. If the connection is a standard connection, the connection details have to match the data server name in the interfaces file entry. If the connection is a SAP Secure User Store connection, this must match the key used to create a user store of encrypted credentials with the `hdbuserstore` utility.

- ❑ `rdb`: This is a placeholder. A value must be provided, but it is not used.

- ❑ `m_user`: This is the maintenance user for the replicate SAP HANA database instance that you created in the previous step.

- ❑ `m_pwd`: This is the maintenance user password for the replicate SAP HANA database.

- ❑ `auser` and `apwd`: These are unused values supplied only to satisfy the syntax of the `create connection` command.

Creating a Replication Server connection to the primary database

The following steps need to be taken:

1. In Replication Server, create a connection to the primary Oracle database:

```
create connection to pds.pdb
using profile rs_rs_to_oracle_ra;standard
set username muser
set password mnt_pwd
with log transfer on, dsi_suspended
go
```

Here,

- ❑ pds: This is the value of the rs_source_ds parameter specified in Replication Agent.

- ❑ pdb: This is the value of the rs_source_db parameter specified in Replication Agent.

- ❑ muser: This is the maintenance user for the primary Oracle database. This user must already exist and have the necessary select permissions in the primary database. See *Primary Database Guide* for more details.

- ❑ mnt_pwd: This is the password for the maintenance user.

2. Use admin show_connections, 'primary' to display the primary connection you created.

Testing the replication

The following steps need to be taken:

1. Connect to the primary Oracle instance as a regular user, rather than as the maintenance user:

    1. At the primary Oracle database, create a table named table1 to be replicated, as shown:

       ```
       CREATE TABLE table1
       (idno NUMBER PRIMARY KEY,
       name VARCHAR2(20));
       ```

    2. Grant permissions to any new or existing object to be replicated in the primary database, as shown:

       ```
       grant all on table1 to public;
       ```

    3. Connect to Replication Agent through isqlisql and mark table1table1table for replication, as shown:

       ```
       pdb_setreptablesetreptabletable1, mark
       go
       ```

    4. In Replication Agent, create a replication definition against the primary Oracle database, as shown:

       ```
       rs_create_repdefrepdeftable1
       go
       ```

5. At the replicate SAP HANA database instance, create a table named `TABLE1`, as shown:

    ```
    CREATE TABLE <tableowner>.TABLE1
    (IDNO INT PRIMARY KEY,
    NAME VARCHAR(20));
    ```

    If an owner is not specified with the table name, the owner of the table `<tableowner>` is the user that is signed on at the time the table is created.

6. Grant permissions to any new or existing object to be replicated in the replicate database so that the Replication Server maintenance user can update this table, as shown:

    ```
    grant all privileges on <tableowner>.TABLE1 to public
    ```

7. Log in to Replication Server, as shown:

    ```
    isql -Usa -Psa_pass -SSAMPLE_RS
    ```

8. Alter the replication definition that you created earlier to point to the correct replicate table, as shown:

    ```
    alter replication definition <repdefname>
    with replicate table named <tableowner>.table1
    go
    ```

9. Create a subscription against the replicate connection, as shown in the following code:

    ```
    create subscription table1_sub
    for <repdefname>
    with replicate at rds.rdb
    without materialization
    go
    ```

10. On the Oracle database, insert the data into the primary `table1` table and commit, as shown here:

    ```
    insert into table1 values (4, 'Crow T. Robot');
    commit;
    ```

11. On the SAP HANA database, verify that the data replicated to the replicate `TABLE1` table, as shown here:

    ```
    SELECT * FROM <tableowner>.TABLE1;
    ```

How it works...

From the latest release of SAP Sybase Replication Server 15.7.1 SP100, data replication to SAP HANA instance is supported for the following listed primary databases:

- Adaptive Server Enterprise (ASE)
- Oracle
- Microsoft SQL Server
- DB2 UDB on Linux, Unix, and Windows

Direct load materialization is also supported between these databases and SAP HANA. Through this, we can materialize data between different primary databases and SAP HANA. Direct load materialization can be used to materialize data in the following ways:

- From Adaptive Server to HANA DB
- From Microsoft SQL Server to HANA DB
- From Oracle to HANA DB
- From DB2 UDB to HANA DB

The architecture of data replication to SAP HANA is shown in the following diagram:

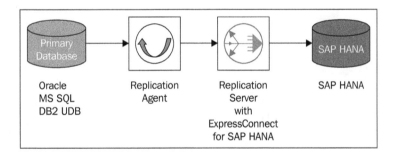

A new connector, ExpressConnect for HANA (ECH), has been introduced to connect to SAP HANA. This connector establishes a direct connection with SAP HANA using the ODBC driver. The ODBC driver is not shipped as a part of SAP Sybase Replication Server. It has to be downloaded separately and installed. ECH is integrated both with the SAP Sybase Replication Server interfaces file and the `hdbuserstore` utility in the SAP HANA client. This enables us to connect to SAP HANA either by adding an entry for the HANA instance in the SAP Sybase Replication Server interfaces file, or by using the `hdbuserstore` HANA client utility to create a **key** (HANA instance) specifying the HANA instance name, host, port, user name, and password. This is so that SAP Sybase Replication Server can access the HANA instance after bypassing the interfaces file and using the `hdbuserstore` key. We can avoid intermediate gateway/ middleware which degrades performance. ECH consists of two Replication Server dynamic link libraries, `libsybhdb` and `libsybhdbodbc`, which are linked with the SAP HANA ODBC driver.

There's more...

The steps mentioned here are to configure replication from Oracle to SAP HANA. Similarly, configuration has to be done for separate source systems, and the steps for configuration steps differ accordingly.

See also

- ▸ Sybase *Replication Server 15.7.1 SP100* at `http://infocenter.sybase.com/help/topic/com.sybase.infocenter.dc32410.1571100/doc/pdf/refman.pdf`
- ▸ Learn more about replicating data to HANA using SAP Sybase Replication Server at `http://scn.sap.com/community/services/blog/2013/06/16/replicating-data-to-hana-using-sap-sybase-replication-server`

3
Modeling

In this chapter, we will cover:

- ▶ Approaching SAP HANA modeling
- ▶ Creating attribute views
- ▶ Creating analytic views
- ▶ Creating calculation views
- ▶ Preparing documents – Auto Documentation
- ▶ Modeling with Information Composer

Introduction

This chapter is full of recipes that deal with creating different types of models in SAP HANA Studio. Once we create schemas and tables and load data to SAP HANA, we can start creating different types of views; that is, attribute, analytic, and calculation views according to our requirements.

Approaching SAP HANA modeling

With data being loaded from any source system, we are now ready to proceed with creating models in a SAP HANA system. So, let us start creating data models in a SAP HANA system. This recipe covers the different types of models that can be created and their importance.

Getting ready

For this, we need **SAP HANA Studio** and **SAP HANA Client** (drivers for SAP HANA) downloaded and installed. These software are available both in 32-bit and 64-bit versions and can be freely downloaded from the Internet.

How to do it...

SAP HANA Studio is used to create models in SAP HANA. There are different types of models, such as attribute views, analytic views, calculation views, and so on. Database tables replicated from different source systems act as the base for these information models. We create attribute views on top of tables. In analytic views, we join fact tables to the attribute views. Database tables or attribute views, analytic views, or calculation views can be included in creating calculation views. Apart from these, we can also create stored procedures. These procedures can also be used in SQLScript-based calculation views.

Attribute views are created for master data modeling. We select master data tables for creating attribute views. Multiple master data tables or text tables can be joined with master data tables to obtain the output.

Analytic views are created using fact tables. These fact tables are joined with the created attribute views to form a star schema. A cube-like structure is created in the analytic view. Measures (the key figures) will be taken from the data foundation (that is, fact table) and then the attribute views will be joined so that the required attributes will be added from these attribute views.

Calculation views are created when the joins in analytic views are not enough to meet the requirements. There are two types of calculation views: graphical and SQL scripting. To meet complex requirements, we may need to write custom SQL code. For this, we go with SQLScript calculation views.

How it works...

SAP HANA Studio is the one-stop tool for developers and technical architects in the SAP HANA landscape for the definition of tables, data models, and to set up and manage various forms of data provisioning in SAP HANA. In this chapter, we will discuss the various modeling capabilities that SAP HANA Studio provides, see a step-by-step process with a hands-on approach to creating models, and perform modeling using practical scenarios. SAP HANA Studio modeling includes attribute views, analytic views, and calculated views. Basically, data in SAP HANA is organized and stored in the form of tables. In these tables, the respective fields are classified either as an attribute or a measure:

> ▶ An attribute in a data-warehouse scenario is called a dimension, and it qualifies something in the data; for example, Country Code, Customer Name, and Country

- A measure is an entity that quantifies something; for example, Order Quantity, Cost, and Sales Amount

SAP HANA models (that is, information views) are based on the join types between them. Master data or fact tables are used to create attribute, analytic, or calculation views. Data output depends on the joins used while creating views. Moreover, the cardinalities between the base tables have to be considered while creating information views.

See also

- *SAP HANA Modeling Guide* at `http://help.sap.com/hana/SAP_HANA_Modeling_Guide_en.pdf`

Creating attribute views

Attribute views are similar to dimensions, but the only difference is that attribute views are reusable components as they are object-oriented throughout the information modeling. In simple terms, these are views on one or multiple tables that can be reused for multiple purposes.

For example, the attribute view `Customers` can show Customer Code, Customer Name, Customer City and other Customer master data. This attribute view can be used in both analytic and calculation views based on the relevance. Generally, attribute views represent the dimension data (master data). But technically, there are no limitations or restrictions as it's definitely possible to create attribute views on transactional data. This recipe explains how to create attribute views.

Getting ready

In order to create attribute views, we must have a database table readily available. We must also possess the MODELER role and SELECT authorization on the schema from which we are accessing the tables. In addition to this, the `_SYS_REPO` user must have the EXECUTE authorization with the GRANT option on the schema.

How to do it...

Let's look at the steps involved in creating attribute views. For any information view to be created, we need a package. Packages are folder-like objects into which information views are organized and structured.

Creating a package

To create a package, go to the **Modeler** perspective and then select **Content** and right-click on **Package**. Optionally, click on **Package** on the **Quick Launch** menu and it creates a package. Based on the naming conventions, the names need to be provided and the package needs to be saved. Each package will be empty soon after creation; we can create an attribute view, analytic view, or calculation view inside the package. The procedure is shown in the following screenshot:

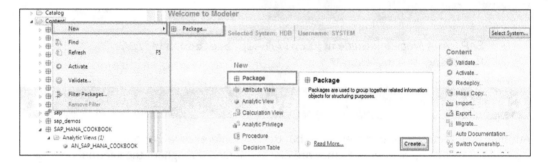

Creating an attribute view

In this section, we will look at the steps involved in creating an attribute view.

Attribute views can be created in two ways: from **Quick Launch** and from the Navigator Pane. Let's have a look at both the methods in detail:

- To create an attribute view from the Navigator Pane, right-click on the package and choose **New** and then click on **Attribute View**.

- To create an attribute view from **Quick Launch**, select **Attribute View** and then click on the **Create** button. An attribute view can be one of several types; the following are the different types:

  - **Standard**: This is an empty attribute view.

  - **Time**: This will create both view and data for time attributes—date, month, and so on.

  - **Copy From**: This is the fastest way to create an attribute view, by leveraging the reusability factor. From an existing attribute view, if the fields are known in the current attribute view, Copy From can be used.

  - **Derived**: This creates a new attribute view from the existing one; the definition may be the same, but the name can be a new one.

The following are the steps to create the attribute view:

1. Click on **Attribute View** with the specification of **Subtype** as **Standard**.

2. Specify the technical name and description.

3. Drag-and-drop the tables in **Data Foundation** to the **Scenario** tab. As soon as we drop a table, we will see the tables in the **Details** tab. There are no limits as such, but we need to add only the required set of tables as performance might be impacted.

4. Join tables if more than one table is included in the data foundation.

5. Select the required fields and they will appear in **Output**.

6. Click on the **Save and Activate** button.

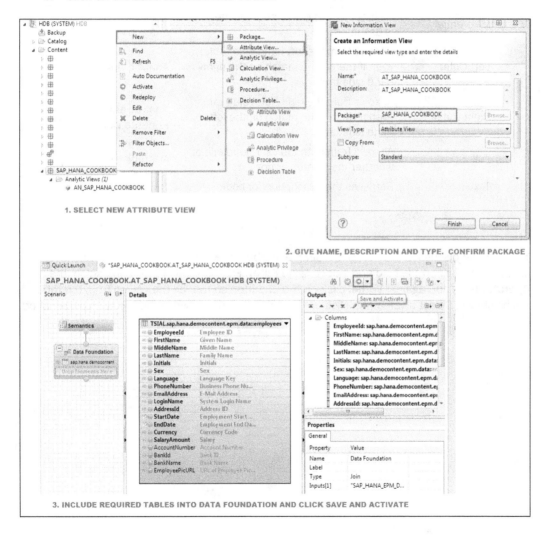

How it works...

Attribute views are used for master data modeling. Multiple master data tables can be included in a single view and joined. When attribute views are called for output, the join engine takes care of processing the data and proving the output.

The different types of joins and where they can be used are described in the following table:

Join Type	Result	Use
Inner	Rows where there is at least one match between both tables	Attribute views and analytic views
Referential	An inner join where referential integrity is assumed	Attribute views and analytic views
Left Outer	All rows from the left-hand side table; even if there is no match on the right-hand side table	Analytic views
Right Outer	All rows from the right-hand side table; even if there is no match on the left-hand side table	Analytic and attribute views
Full	All rows from both tables, regardless of whether they match or not	Attribute views
Text	Retrieves the description for code	To join text tables

There's more...

The example discussed previously is a simple attribute view. We can also create field-level filters. Right-click on the field and select **Apply Filter**. From the pop-up window, select the **Operator** type, and against **Value**, click on the **...** button so that all the values from the table will be shown. Select a value and click on the **OK** button as shown in the following screenshot:

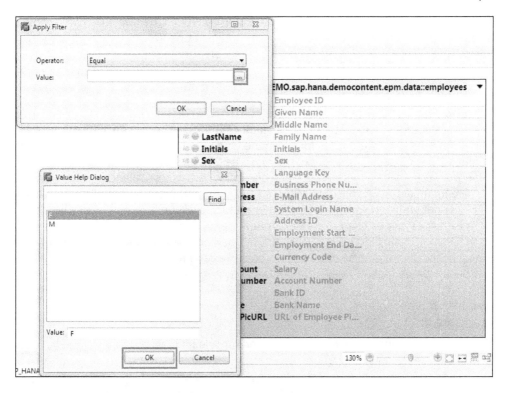

Now, as we can see, a yellow funnel for the field will be visible, indicating that the filter has been applied:

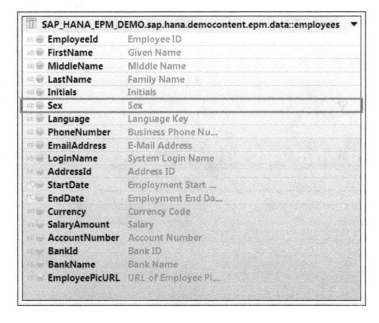

An attribute view can also be created as Derived or Copy From. When we select an attribute view as a copy, it inherits all the properties of the original attribute. The new attribute view can be modified even after creation. When we create an attribute view as Derived, the newly created attribute view cannot be modified after creation. When the original attribute view is modified, changes will be applicable to the newly created attribute view.

We can also create time attribute views. These are used when time data has to be generated. On selecting **Generate Time Data** from the **Quick Launch** screen, we can create time-related data. We can select a range of data for which the time data has to be generated along with the granularity. For example, if we input the range as 2011 to 2013 with granularity as day, data for every day will be generated. We can also select the type of calendar used for this; that is, Gregorian or Fiscal. This data will be stored in the _SYS_BI schema. Based on the type of calendar and granularity selected, different tables will be generated along with the data. These tables can be used to create attribute views. While creating the attribute view, the type has to be selected as Time. This attribute view can be joined to other analytic views by joining based on the date field; for a given date, we can have time data with different levels of data such as year, month, week, and day.

See also

- Learn more about SAP HANA information models for master data at http://scn.sap.com/community/hana-in-memory/blog/2013/05/06/sap-hana-information-models-for-master-data-attribute-view-series1

- A video that explains attribute view creation in SAP HANA (using single and multiple tables) is available at http://scn.sap.com/docs/DOC-26093

- A video that explains about hierarchies and calculated columns in an attribute view is available at http://www.sapanalyticsguru.com/index.php/sap-hana/50-sap-hana-e-learning-hierarchies-and-calculated-columns-in-attribute-view

- A video that explains the creation of the time attribute view is available at http://www.sapanalyticsguru.com/index.php/sap-hana/51-sap-hana-e-learning-how-to-create-time-attribute-view

Creating analytic views

An analytic view is a modeling view in which the dimension tables are joined with the fact table that contains transaction data; that is, measures. Variables can be created in these analytic views. When a fact table is joined with dimension tables, it forms a cube-like structure, so analysis gives us meaningful joined data.

Getting ready

Similar to the attribute views, in order to create analytic views, we should have fact tables loaded with data in a schema. The _SYS_REPO user must have the SELECT authorization on the table with the GRANT option. Otherwise, the activation of the analytic view fails with an authorization error.

How to do it...

Like attribute view, analytic views can also be created from either the **Quick Launch** screen or the Navigator Pane. In this section, we will see how to create an analytic view from the Navigator Pane:

1. Right-click on the package in the Navigator view and go to **New | Analytic View** as shown in the following screenshot:

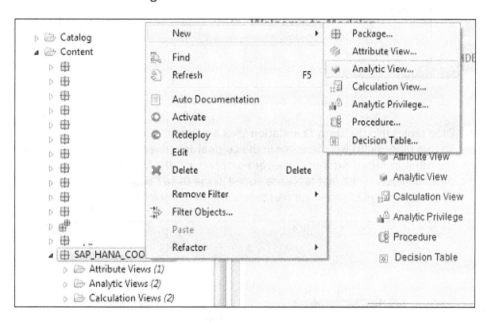

2. Provide a technical name and description as shown here:

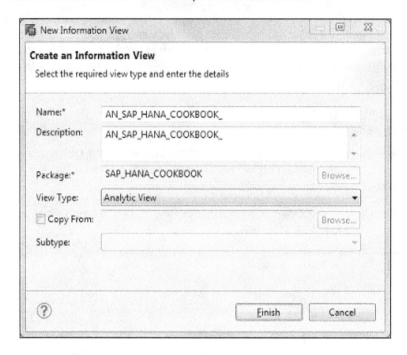

3. Drop tables into the **Data Foundation** level and add the required fields to **Output** so that those fields will be visible in the **Logical Join** level and can be joined with the attribute views. Attribute views are dropped into the **Logical Join** level, the join between fields of the fact table are added in the **Data Foundation** level, and the fields in the attribute view are created as shown in the following screenshot:

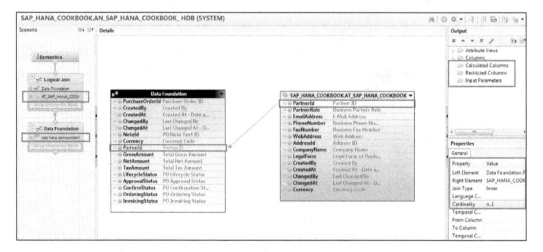

4. In the next level (that is, **Semantics**), all fields are identified and confirmed to be either attributes or measures, as shown in the following screenshot. For measures, the aggregation is to be set accordingly.

How it works...

Analytic views are processed by the **Online Analytical Processing** (**OLAP**) engine. When we have multiple dimensions to be joined to the fact table (which has measures), we go with an analytic view. We create attribute views for each dimension table. We join these attribute views to the fact table. Based on the join and the cardinality we have set, we obtain the results. As mentioned before, the OLAP engine is responsible for processing analytic views. We can also create calculated measures in analytic views. These will be calculated at runtime and hence saves memory space as we don't need to store extra information. These values are calculated easily, and as everything runs in memory, we get the results without any lag.

There's more...

We can also create filters on the fields in analytic views. The process of doing this is similar to that of creating filters in attribute views. There are a few more options such as **Calculated Columns**, **Restricted Columns**, and **Input Parameters**. Calculated Columns are those where we create new columns with a formula based on the columns that are already available. Restricted Columns are those where we restrict columns based on some particular value of attributes.

Moreover, analytic views can be accessed by **SAP BusinessObjects Explorer** (**SAP BO Explorer**) and **SAP Lumira** directly.

See also

▸ A video that explains the usage of calculated columns in an analytic view is available at http://www.saphana.com/docs/DOC-3126

▸ Learn more about SAP HANA information models for master data at http://scn.sap.com/community/hana-in-memory/blog/2013/05/06/sap-hana-information-models-for-master-data-analytic-views-series3

Creating calculation views

Calculation views are more advanced models in SAP HANA that are defined when requirements cannot be met with attribute and analytic views. For example, with calculation views, we can extract the required measures from more than one transaction table in the result, which is not possible with an analytic view. As well as this feature, we can define calculations at different layers and also use advanced SQL logic in calculation views. We can create joins, projections, unions, and aggregations in calculation views. This recipe explains how to create different types of calculation views.

Getting ready

Calculation views can be created in two ways:

▸ Using GUI (Graphical User Interface)

▸ Using SQLScript (native SQL or CE functions)

Any combination of the following objects can be a part of the calculation view data foundation:

▸ Tables

▸ Column views

▸ Attribute views

▸ Analytic views

▸ Calculation views

We can create the following objects while defining a calculation view:

- ▶ Attributes
- ▶ Measures
- ▶ Hierarchies
- ▶ Calculated measures/attributes
- ▶ Counters
- ▶ Variables
- ▶ Input parameters

How to do it...

In this section, we will see how to create a calculation view in SAP HANA Studio. The source for the calculation is the analytic view (**AN_SAP_HANA_COOKBOOK**) created in the *Creating analytic views* recipe. This analytic view has sales order data; here, we will join this with product information, which is available in the table, to perform meaningful analysis.

Creation of a calculation view using GUI

Follow these steps:

1. Right-click on the package and go to **New** | **Calculation View**:

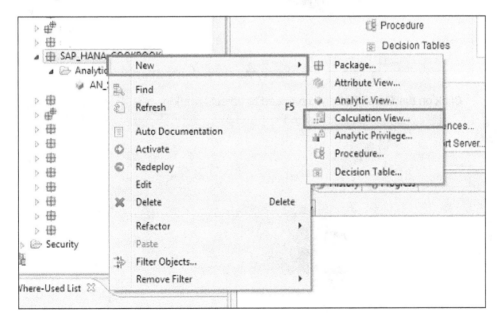

2. Provide the technical name, description, and the type of calculation view that needs to be created (**Graphical** or **SQL Script**) as shown in the following screenshot. A schema for currency conversion has to be selected if we want to apply/use any currency conversion. The schema selected here should contain the currency-related tables (such as TCURR, TCURV, and TCURN).

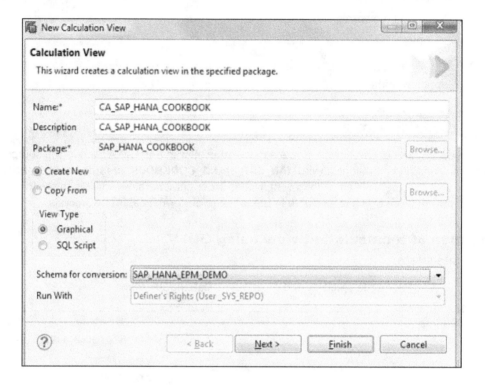

Click on the **Finish** button to proceed to object creation.

3. Now we have to select sources for the calculation view. Sources can be tables; column views in a schema; or attribute, analytic, or calculation views in packages, or a combination of these. Select the required objects and move them to the right-hand-side area, as shown in the following screenshot:

Click on **Finish** to enter into the design area of the calculation view.

4. The calculation view design area contains three sections. The left-hand side contains the source, output, and the objects we use from the **Tools Palette**. The middle section shows details about the object we select in the left-hand side. The right-hand side contains the fields we have selected for output and the additional objects that we can create based on the output fields. This is shown in the following screenshot:

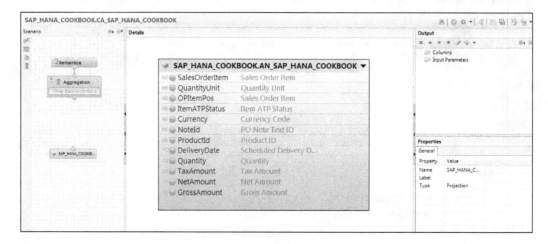

5. Now, if we want to add additional objects as sources at a later stage, we can use the table button available above the middle area, as shown in the following screenshot:

6. Look for the objects we want using the search option and click on **OK** to add them to the calculation view, as shown in the following screenshot:

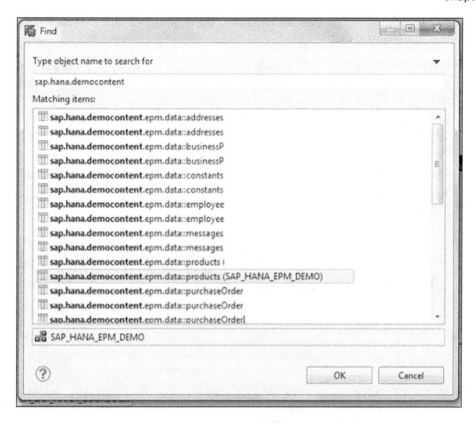

7. We can see that the table on the left-hand side appears as follows:

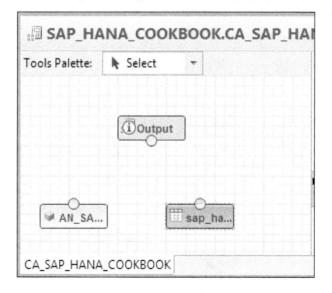

To start building the calculation view, we can select the options available in **Tools Palette**. We have the following options:

- ▸ **Union**: This is used to combine data from two or more sources. It works as "union all", which brings all the records from both the sources together. This is the preferred join when sources are analytic views.

- ▸ **Join**: This is used to join two or more sources to get the result. We can use inner, left outer, right outer, and text join here. Based on the join type we select, the result data set varies.

- ▸ **Projection**: This is used to filter the fields or select the required fields from the source.

- ▸ **Aggregation**: This is used to aggregate the measures based on specific attributes (master data). The supported aggregations here are sum, min, and max.

We can use results of projection, union, join, and aggregation as sources for projection, union, join, and aggregation.

The source object for projection and aggregation is a single entity. The source objects for joins are two entities. For unions, the source objects can be more than two entities.

Follow the given steps:

1. As our requirement is to join an analytic view with the PRODUCTS table, we will use Join. Before we apply Join, we use Projection on the analytic view and Products to select the required fields for output.

2. Now open **Tools Palette** and select the required objects. We can also rename the objects to give them more meaningful names.

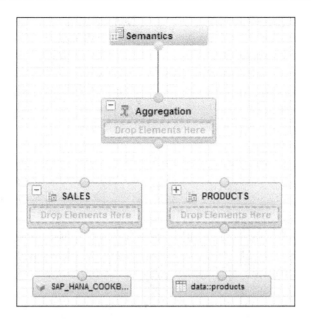

3. Now join the source objects to the projects we have selected. To join, move the mouse to the source. This shows an arrow mark on the right-hand side. Select the arrow and drag-and-drop it onto the target as shown in the following screenshot:

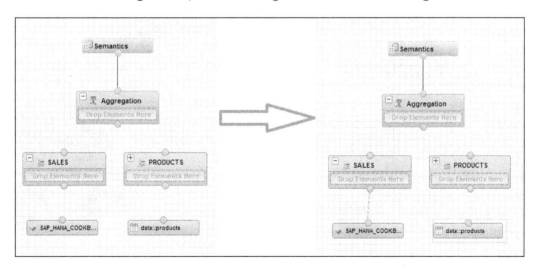

4. Perform the same steps for PRODUCTS as well. Now, to select the required fields from the source, select the projection that displays the list of available objects in the middle area. Right-click on the objects we want for output and select **Add To Output** as shown in the following screenshot:

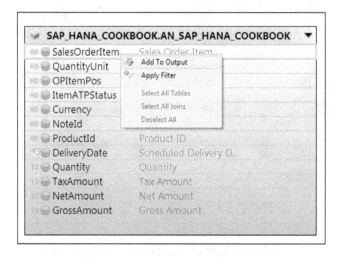

5. Once we add the fields to the output, we can select the fields under the **Columns** folder on the right-hand side as shown here:

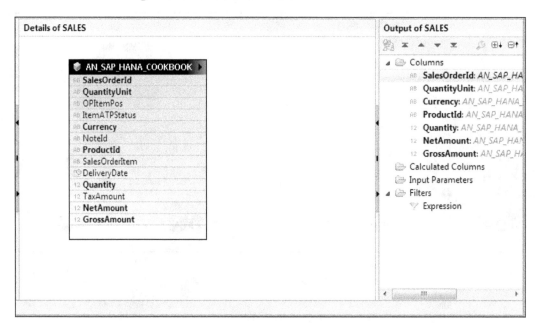

6. We use **Join** from **Tools Palette** to join both the projections of analytic views. **Join Type** will have to be changed to **Left Outer** as we are joining transaction data with master data, and **Cardinality** will be **N:1** as shown in the following screenshot. We can change the join type in the **Property** area. The joining field will be common for the two sources.

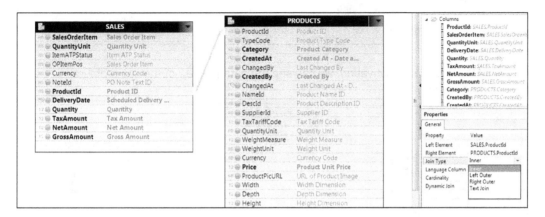

7. Once the join is established, select the fields for output using the same process we followed earlier (right-click on the field and click on **Add To Output**), as shown in the following screenshot:

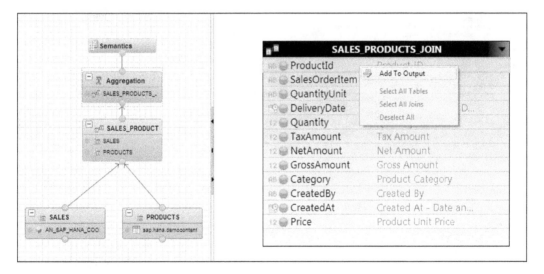

8. Once the required fields are added to the output as attributes and measures, we can go ahead with the activation of the calculation view. Use the green arrow symbol to do this. We can see the status of activation as shown in the following screenshot:

9. After successful activation, we can see the data preview of the same object as shown:

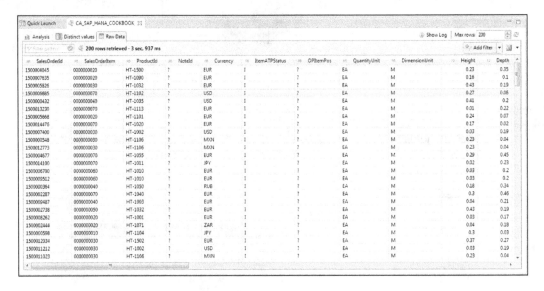

Creation of a calculation view using SQLScript (native SQL or CE functions)

The other method of creating a calculation view is using SQLScript. We can use native SQL or **Calculation Engine** (**CE**) functions, as they are processed by a calculation engine. Using CE functions optimizes query execution cost as compared to the usage of SQLScript. At the time of writing this book, SAP HANA supports the following CE functions: CE_COLUMN_TABLE: This is used to read data from the Column table

- ▸ CE_JOIN_VIEW: This is used to read data from attribute views

- ▸ CE_OLAP_VIEW: This is used to read data from analytic views

- ▸ CE_CALC_VIEW: This is used to read data from calculation views

- ▸ CE_JOIN: This is used to read data from more than one source based on the inner join

- ▸ CE_LEFT_OUTER_JOIN: This is used to read data from more than one source based on the left outer join

- ▸ CE_RIGHT_OUTER: This is used to read data from more than one source based on the right outer join

- ▸ CE_UNION_ALL: This is used to read all the data from more than one source using the UNION ALL function

- ▸ CE_CALC: This is used to calculate new fields in the result data set

- ▸ CE_PROJECTION: This is used to select the required fields from the source based on the requirement

- ▸ CE_AGGREGATION: This is used to aggregate the measure based on the group of attributes

- ▸ CE_CONVERSION: This is used to perform currency conversion

Let's say we want to create a calculation view that reads data from an analytic view. We can achieve this using the CE_OLAP_VIEW function, which is used to read the data from an analytic view.

The creation of a new calculation view will follow the same procedure as explained earlier in step 2 of the *Creation of a calculation view using GUI* section, except we select **SQL Script** instead of **Graphical**, as shown in the following screenshot:

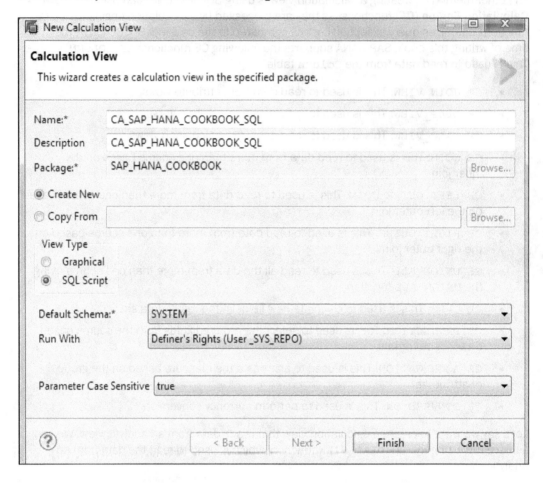

Now, click on **Finish** to enter the design area of the calculation view, as shown:

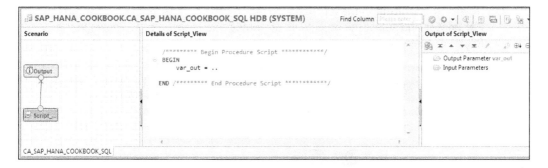

Follow these steps to create a calculation view using CE functions:

1. Type in `var_out` (click on **Script_View** on the left-hand side to get the preceding screen).

2. Define the input and output parameters based on the code.

3. Select the attributes and measures from the output area.

   The following code is the syntax to read data from an analytic view using `CE_OLAP_VIEW`:

   ```
   Var_out = CE_OLAP_VIEW
   ("_SYS_BIC"."SAP_HANA_COOKBOOK/AN_SAP_HANA_COOKBOOK",["SalesOrderI
   d","ProductId",
   "QuantityUnit","Currency","Quantity","GrossAmount","NetAmount"]);
   ```

   While defining the output parameter, the names and data types should match the source objects. This is illustrated in the following screenshot:

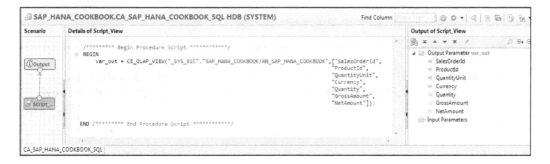

4. Now click on **Output** in the left-hand side to see the objects defined in **Output Parameter** and select the objects as attributes and measures, as shown in the following screenshot:

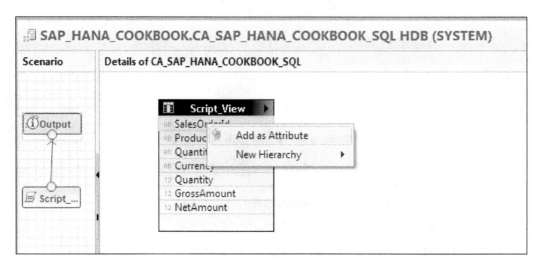

5. We can go ahead and activate other attributes and measures using the green arrow button. The following screenshot shows the activation status:

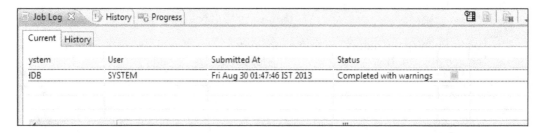

6. We can also see the data preview after a successful job completion. Right-click on the object and select **Data Preview**. The following screenshot shows the data preview:

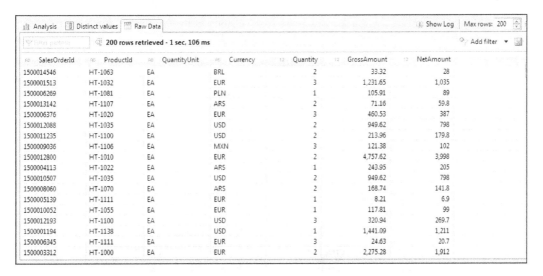

The same result can be achieved using the following native SQL statement:

```
Var_out = SELECT
"SalesOrderId","ProductId","QuantityUnit","Currency","Quantity","G
rossAmount","NetAmount" from
"_SYS_BIC"."SAP_HANA_COOKBOOK/AN_SAP_HANA_COOKBOOK";
```

The performance-wise calculation view using the graphical approach gives best results, while using native SQL does not.

How it works...

When a calculation view is activated, the system creates a column view in the `_SYS_BIC` schema. This column view is exposed to reporting tools. The created calculation view is not directly available for reporting. If we want to enable this and make the calculation view available for reporting, under the **Semantics** section, we should enable **MultiDimensional Reporting**. When this is enabled, the execution occurs using CE functions in the index server at the database level.

See also

▸ Learn more about creating and using HANA native scripted calculation views in SAP HANA Cloud at `http://scn.sap.com/community/developer-center/cloud-platform/blog/2013/07/10/creating-and-using-hana-native-scripted-calculation-view-in-sap-hana-cloud`

▸ *Building Advanced Data Models with SAP HANA* at `http://www.sdn.sap.com/irj/sdn/go/portal/prtroot/docs/library/uuid/6056911a-07cc-2e10-7a8a-ffa9b8cf579c?overridelayout=true`

▸ Learn about building an analytic and calculation view from the Wikipedia HANA tables for use with SAP Lumira at `http://scn.sap.com/community/developer-center/hana/blog/2013/07/19/building-an-analytic-calculation-view-from-the-hana-tables-for-use-with-sap-lumira`

▸ A video that explains the creation of calculation views with the graphical interface is available at `http://www.saphana.com/docs/DOC-2262`

Preparing documents – Auto Documentation

For the work we do or the objects we build, it is very important that everything be documented for future reference. In any project, the documentation part is very critical, which includes documenting each detail about the creation of objects, its functionality, and so on. Usually, documentation is a manual process, but in SAP HANA, there is an option that helps auto-document all the models we have created. This recipe helps us understand how to use the Auto Documentation option in SAP HANA.

How to do it...

Auto documentation can be performed from the **Quick Launch** screen or the Navigator Pane. If we choose **Quick Launch**, we have to select the package manually. From the Navigator Pane, right-click on the package; and from the context menu, select **Auto Documentation** as shown in the following screenshot. This enables us to auto-document the package we selected. Let us see how to auto-document with **Model Details** and **Model List** and the difference between the reports they generate.

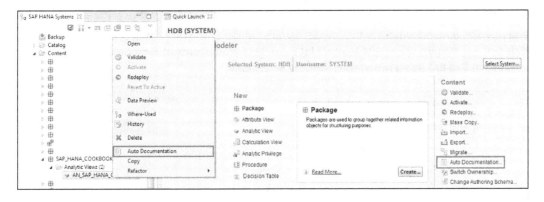

Model Details

Click on **Auto Documentation** from the **Quick Launch** screen or right-click on the package that needs to be documented and then select **Auto Documentation**. Now, from the dropdown against **Select Content Type**, select **Model Details**. Select all the required packages and add them to the target section. Browse to the target location from the lower part of the screen and click on the **Finish** button as shown in the following screenshot:

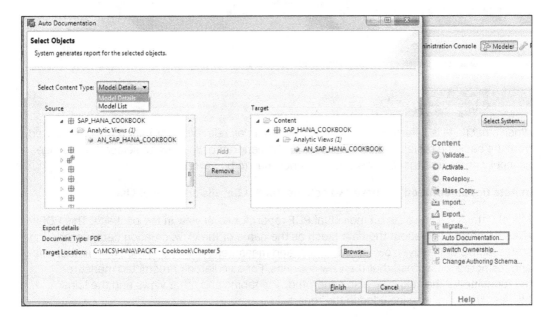

Model List

The steps to auto-document with a model list are similar to the preceding procedure. The only difference is that we will select **Model List** from the **Select Content Type** dropdown. The steps involved in this are as shown in the following screenshot:

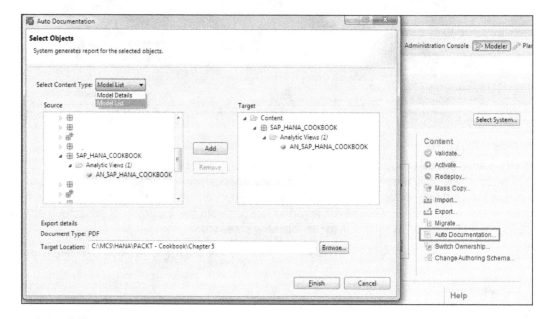

How it works...

When a package is selected for auto documentation, all relevant information will be collected from the backend tables and a PDF report will be generated. We have to select the package as input and browse the folder where the report has to be saved.

In **Auto Documentation**, we have two options: **Model Details** and **Model List**.

Model Details will generate an individual PDF report for each view in the package. This PDF gives us information about the data [such as the name of the view, creation date, description, status (active or inactive), owner, attributes, and measures (all types—direct, calculated, and restricted measures)] that the view contains. For calculated or restricted measures, the formulae for the fields are also generated. The tables and other views and the joins between them are also included in the report.

Model List will generate a single PDF per package. This PDF will contain the list of views in each package. The metadata about the package will be displayed, which includes name, description, system name, and owner of the package. A list with the name of the view, type (attribute/analytic/calculation), owner (who created it), and the status (active/inactive) will also be displayed.

Modeling with Information Composer

SAP HANA Information Composer can also be called Information Composer for short. This tool is intended mainly for modeling purposes by power users and authors. Power users are defined as those business users who have the capability to create new reporting elements for themselves, and authors are those users who can additionally share those new reports with other users. This recipe shows us how to create models using Information Composer.

Getting ready

Information Composer can be accessed in the browser by entering a web address. The web address will be similar to the one shown here:

```
http://<server name>:8080/IC or https://<server name>:8443/IC
```

To start working with Information Composer, Microsoft Silverlight has to be installed and activated as an add-on to the web browser.

How to do it...

In this section, we will see how to upload data into SAP HANA and learn about data cleansing. After data is loaded, information views can be created.

Uploading data

We can upload data into SAP HANA using Information Composer and create models on top of that. The following file types are supported for data loading using Information Composer:

- ▸ Comma-delimited files (CSV)
- ▸ Microsoft Excel files (`.xls` or `.xslx`)
- ▸ Clipboard

The steps involved in loading data using Information Composer will be discussed in the following sections.

Selecting a data source and loading data into Information Composer

After logging in to Information Composer, select the **Upload** option on the home screen. Then select **Start**. Now, on the left-hand side of the screen, we can see three menu items: **Source**, **Classify**, and **Finish**:

- ▸ **Source**: This is used to select a data source and then load data
- ▸ **Classify**: This is for classification of data columns into attributes and measures
- ▸ **Finish**: This is used for finally saving data into SAP HANA

Now click on **Source** and select the **Data** radio button from **File System**. Browse the file and select a worksheet if the selected Excel has multiple sheets. The point to be remembered in this context is that we can only load one sheet's data at a time. The reason is Information Composer will automatically create a table in SAP HANA for the file we upload. When we take data from the Clipboard, it has to be in such a way that Information Composer has to recognize rows and columns in that data. Hence, it should be in a structured manner, similar to the data that comes in an Excel spreadsheet.

There will be an option to load data with column headers. Selecting this enables us to load column headers too. Then, clicking on **Upload** loads data to Information Composer and a confirmation message appears. We can also see a sample data preview on the screen.

Once data is successfully uploaded, several options will be enabled, such as **Data Cleansing** on the right-hand side and **Classify** on the left-hand side. The data loaded is not yet stored in the SAP HANA database. This data is temporarily held in the Information Composer session. All the fields are treated as literals, as we haven't classified the data. There is one more option at the bottom, the **Data Summary View** button. This gives us the top five values of each column based on the occurrences in the table.

Data cleansing

Data cleansing is not mandatory and depends from scenario to scenario. If data cleansing is required, perform the following step. Otherwise, we can proceed with the next step; that is, classifying data columns into attributes and measures:

> ▸ Click on **CLEANSE DATA** in the top right-hand side of the screen for data cleansing. The options for data cleansing depend on the data we have uploaded. But by default, we will always have Merge and Change values.

Merging values

This is useful when we have to merge data based on the values of a single column. For example, let us consider that we have data for five sales organizations. The number of values for three sales orgs is similar, but the record count for the other two sales orgs varies by a huge difference. Hence, we might think of merging two different sales orgs and viewing the results. Select the sales org that we want to make the source. The other sales org will be displayed on the screen. Drag the sales org that has to be merged into the source sales org. Immediately, the results vary based on both of the merged sales orgs. If we wish to revert to the original results, we will have the **Undo** option, which helps to achieve it in a single click.

Changing values

This is useful when there is a need to change the value of data. To do this, let us see the results based on month. There might be chances that month names are loaded in different ways—August and Aug. With values being different, results will be displayed separately for both the values, though it conveys data for the same month. Now we can change Aug to August or August to Aug, as per our convenience. After we make the change, data for both values will be merged and displayed as a single entity.

To change values, select a value that has to be changed and click on **Change**. Enter the new value and click on **OK**. The value will now be changed and the data will get adjusted based on the values.

Classification of data columns into attributes and measures

Now that the data has been cleansed, we can proceed with identifying measures in the given data set. As discussed earlier, the **Classify** button will be enabled only after successfully loading data into Information Composer. From the left-hand side of the screen, select **Classify**. This gives us an option to select which columns have to act as measures. A checkbox will be present to select the columns. The selected columns act as measures, on which calculations can be performed. By default, all the columns will be treated as attributes. Only the selected columns act as measures and will be available for calculations. Soon after loading data, based on the data in all the columns, Information Composer proposes fields for selecting them as measures.

Saving data into SAP HANA

Click on **Finish** from the menu on the left-hand side. Now we have to enter a technical name and description. The technical name we enter will be the name of the data source, which can be used in SAP HANA for creating views. There are two more options at the bottom of the screen, **Share this data with other users** and **Start a new Information View based on this data**. As these are checkboxes again, we have to select an option according to our requirement.

Selecting **Share this data with other users** will enable the data to be shared across different users. All the users who have the IC_PUBLIC role in SAP HANA can access this data. If this checkbox is not selected, the created view behaves like a private one, which can be accessed by us alone.

Selecting **Start a new Information View based on this data** will start a new compose screen with this view as soon as we click on **Finish**. We can create a new view and combine data from this window.

Composing information views

After loading data into Information Composer, we can start creating views. Information views created in Information Composer will have two sources of data. These can be combined based on Join, Union, or custom mapping according to the requirement. The following are the steps involved in creating information views in Information Composer:

- ▸ Selecting data sources—Source A and Source B
- ▸ Combining data
- ▸ Refining the data (which includes removing unnecessary columns, creating calculated columns, and data cleansing)
- ▸ Saving the view in SAP HANA and publishing

For creating information views, from the home screen of Information Composer, select **Compose**. For uploading data, we have selected **Upload** earlier. On selecting **Compose**, we will get five menu items on the left-hand side: **Source A**, **Source B**, **Combine**, **Refine**, and **Finish**. Each option is related to a step. Let us see in detail how to perform all these steps.

Selecting data sources – Source A and Source B

From the menu on the left-hand side of the screen, select **Source A**. At the bottom of the screen, we will have several options that can be selected as the type of source. A search box is present to start searching for the objects if we know the name. The search works in such a way that the search string will be considered only at the beginning of the objects. For example, if our analytic view in SAP HANA is AN_SALES_VIEW, the search string should start with AN. If we search with SALES, it doesn't show any results. There will be options to view objects based on attribute views / analytic views / calculation views / user data. Click on the information view and it acts as Source A now. Similarly, select the data source for Source B. Data preview is possible for the selected data source so that we can confirm the data after selecting the source.

Combining data

After selecting the data sources, the next step is to combine data. Information Composer will propose a combination of data based on the column headers and the data in it. We can also proceed with our own combination settings, ignoring the combinations proposed by the system. Data can be combined in three ways: Union, Join, and manual mappings.

While we are doing combination settings on our own, we will have the options of Join, Union, and manual mappings. The combination type should be selected appropriately, otherwise it will end up giving incorrect results. Let's have a look at these three tasks:

- ▸ **Join**: This is usually used to combine data with measures from one source with the data of an other source that has more attributes to qualify the data further. Joins match rows from both sources based on the condition we define for the join. Inner join is applied by default by Information Composer when we select Join. Left-outer and right-outer joins are also supported by Information Composer. These can be selected from the **Advanced Operations** link.

- ▶ **Union**: This is usually used to combine two sets of measures that have a higher number of attributes in common. Union adds the rows from the second source to the data of the first source while matching the columns.

- ▶ **Manual mapping**: We go with manual mapping when there are no fields identified by Information Composer for Join or Union. In this case, we select the fields manually and continue with manual mapping with advanced options. Join and Union provide basic or simple kinds of mappings. On selecting the manual mapping option, we will have two sources of data: one on the left-hand side and the other on the right-hand side. Fields from both the sources are selected against each other. After the fields are mapped, we proceed by clicking on **OK** and complete the data combination step.

Refining the data

In most cases, refining of data is not required as data will be cleansed while loading. Field classification can be checked in this step and creating new calculated fields can be done at this level. If there are any attributes or measures to be calculated, we can create them here and save them to the SAP HANA view. The technical name, description, and formula has to be given for creating calculated fields.

Saving the view to SAP HANA and publishing

As the last step, we just save and publish the view.

How it works...

Information Composer is a web-based tool that is used for uploading data into SAP HANA and so you can start modeling by creating information views. As stated, this tool is for end users such as business users and authors; therefore, we don't need much technical expertise to use Information Composer. It is a self-service tool. We can perform data acquisition and data manipulation using Information Composer. We can load, view, and clean data according to our requirements and then create physical tables in the SAP HANA system. We can then create information views by selecting two or more objects, thereby enabling the SAP BusinessObjects reporting tools to consume the same. After uploading the data, we can combine it with the existing information views and create new ones directly in Information Composer. These created views can be stored back in SAP HANA and can be used as private or shared as well. Information Composer has basic modeling capabilities, just as SAP HANA Studio. This can be done outside the organization also as this is a web-based tool. Now we will see how to perform different tasks with Information Composer: uploading data, composing (creating views), saving views back to SAP HANA, and sharing views with others.

There's more...

Apart from uploading and creating information views in Information Composer, there are options to preview the data we loaded and the created information views. These options are provided from Information Composer's end because at some point of time in the future, we might need to modify the view. For these actions, we have two tools in Information Composer: **My Data** and **My Information Views**.

My Data

In the initial screen where data is uploaded, to the left-hand side of the screen, there will be an area named **My Data**. This helps in viewing data that is uploaded, published to SAP HANA, and also the data that is being uploaded; that is, in progress.

There is a filter that we can use to view different sets of data. The filter contains the following values:

▸ **Public user data**: This shows all the data that is uploaded to SAP HANA and shared by all users, including ourselves. Only the data that is uploaded with the **Share this data with other users** option will be available here.

▸ **Private user data**: This shows the data that is uploaded by that user. Being private, we cannot see the data of other users.

▸ **Draft user data**: This shows all the data that is uploaded but not saved to SAP HANA.

The data uploaded into Information Composer and not yet saved/published can be edited from this screen. We can rename, delete, and share this data. This data can also be exported to CSV files. Views that are already published can be renamed or shared. Views that are already shared cannot be edited, but can be exported. The **My Data** screen can be primarily used to refresh existing data. We can do this by selecting the appropriate data set and then clicking on **Refresh Data**. After clicking on this, we have to specify a data source. Now select **Update**; this loads the data to SAP HANA.

My Information Views

When the COMPOSE function is selected, on the left-hand side, an area will be displayed named **My Information Views**. This is similar to **My Data**, except that in **My Data**, data is listed, and in this area, views are listed. Even here, all the views will be listed by default; filters are available for draft, private, and public models. Draft models are those that are finished but not yet saved. Private models are those that are finished and saved. Being private, these will be accessible only to the user who has created them. Public models are those that are created and shared with others by selecting **Share this data with other users**.

Other properties of the views remain the same as data; that is, we can only rename/share the views that are published but not shared. Views that are published and shared can only be exported.

See also

- *SAP HANA Information Composer – Installation and Configuration Guide* available at `http://www.google.co.in/url?sa=t&rct=j&q=&esrc=s&source=web&cd=1&cad=rja&ved=0CCoQFjAA&url=http%3A%2F%2Fhelp.sap.com%2Fhana%2FSAP_HANA_Information_Composer_Installation_Guide_en.pdf&ei=DRaXUv9jhpKuB_SXgYAB&usg=AFQjCNFA7V6YcFefRM64T7zG9YfDuqkhFw&sig2=kuPOlDs0kpZT2cmRFkFkAA&bvm=bv.57155469,d.bmk`

- *SAP HANA Information Composer – End User Guide* available at `http://www.google.co.in/url?sa=t&rct=j&q=&esrc=s&source=web&cd=1&cad=rja&ved=0CCoQFjAA&url=http%3A%2F%2Fhelp.sap.com%2Fhana%2FSAP_HANA_Information_Composer_End_User_Guide_en.pdf&ei=HBaXUsvFMIetrAfO5YCoDw&usg=AFQjCNFvFmjxxDE_BEl6_IyLlKgrFEzFtw&sig2=62zOFuBFhUProDsrc2wl4w&bvm=bv.57155469,d.bmk`

- SAP Note: 1627904

 The links for the mentioned guides may change when a new version of tools is available in the market. Hence, search for the latest version of guides with the key terms mentioned in the *See also* section.

4

Reporting

In this chapter, we will cover:

- ▶ The reporting layer on top of SAP HANA
- ▶ Connecting reporting tools to SAP HANA
- ▶ Creating reports using SAP BusinessObjects Web Intelligence
- ▶ Creating reports using SAP BusinessObjects Explorer
- ▶ Creating reports using SAP BusinessObjects Dashboards/Xcelsius
- ▶ Creating reports using SAP BusinessObjects Analysis for OLAP
- ▶ Creating reports using Microsoft Excel
- ▶ Creating reports in SAP Lumira

Introduction

For an organization or a decision maker, it is very important to analyze data before making a decision. They may have tons of information, but everything is vain if it is does not help them make the right decisions at the right time. In SAP HANA, we take raw data from different source systems and transform it into meaningful information. This can be consumed by a reporting tool, hence, helping in decision making. This chapter deals with reporting on top of SAP HANA.

The reporting layer on top of SAP HANA

Until now, we have been loading data successfully into SAP HANA, it is now ready to be consumed by the end users for analysis purpose. At the time of writing this, the SAP BusinessObjects BI platform, SAP Crystal Reports, SAP Lumira (formerly known as SAP Visual Intelligence), and Microsoft Excel were supported by SAP. Hence in this chapter, we will look into how to report using the SAP BO tools and Excel.

How to do it...

All the required drivers such as JDBC, and ODBC, ODBO for SAP HANA come as a part of the SAP HANA clients. Installing the SAP HANA clients by running the `.exe` file will make all the drivers available on the PC and we can connect reporting tools to SAP HANA. The SAP HANA clients are free to download and can be downloaded from the following link:

```
https://hanadeveditionsapicl.hana.ondemand.com/hanadevedition/
```

Clients are available for Windows and Linux, for both 32- and 64-bit versions. The client has to be downloaded and installed accordingly to the OS and its version.

How it works...

Different reporting tools such as SAP BO Web Intelligence, SAP BO Explorer, and SAP Lumira are connected to SAP HANA using different connectivity options. Drivers used by each reporting tool will be different. For example, the SAP BusinessObjects tools use the JDBC/ODBC driver, Excel uses ODBO, and so on. These drivers act as intermediates between SAP HANA and the client reporting tools when presenting data to users. The choice of reporting tool depends on the type of reports that are required. For example, if a detailed level of reporting with interactive interface to the users is required, we go with Web Intelligence. If a high level of reporting with What-If Analysis is required, we go with Dashboard.

There's more...

To access ODBC connectivity with SAP HANA; after installing the SAP HANA clients, System DSN has to be added in ODBC Data Source Administrator in the Control Panel.

▶ A list of supported clients for SAP HANA can be found in SAP Note 1577218, which is available at `https://websmp130.sap-ag.de/sap(bD1lbiZjPTAwMQ==)/bc/bsp/sno/ui_entry/entry.htm?param=69765F6D6F64653D3030312669765F7361706E6F7465735F6E756D6265723D3135373731323826`

Connecting reporting tools to SAP HANA

In this recipe, we will see how to connect different reporting tools to SAP HANA.

Getting ready

With different reporting tools available to consume data on top of SAP HANA, these are connected in different ways. As discussed earlier, all middleware drivers are provided by SAP in the form of SAP HANA Clients. This has to be installed in order to configure additional settings so that the SAP BO tools can be connected to SAP HANA.

As a prerequisite, we need to install SAP HANA Clients to proceed in order to create connections. We will see connection configurations for ODBC and SAP BO Explorer.

How to do it...

The ODBC configuration can be completed through the following steps:

1. After installing SAP HANA Clients, go to **Control Panel** and open **Administrative Tools**.

2. Select **Data Sources (ODBC)** from the list of **Administrative Tools**, as shown in the following screenshot:

Component Services	14-07-2009 10:27	Shortcut	2 KB
Computer Management	14-07-2009 10:24	Shortcut	2 KB
Data Sources (ODBC)	14-07-2009 10:23	Shortcut	2 KB
Event Viewer	14-07-2009 10:24	Shortcut	2 KB

3. Navigate to the **System DSN** tab and click on **Add**. From the list of ODBC drivers available, select the driver that is provided by **SAP AG**, as shown in the following screenshot:

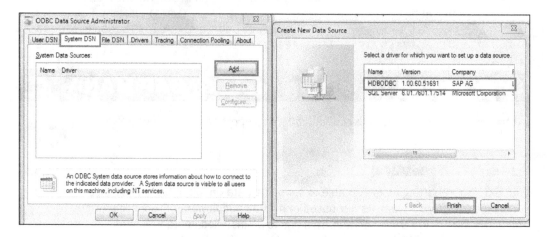

4. Enter **Data Source Name**, server address, and port number, and then click on **Connect**. It will prompt for a user and password. Enter the details of the SAP HANA user and password and click on **OK**, as shown in the following screenshot. By doing this, we complete the connection to SAP HANA using the ODBC driver. This connection can be used to connect from different tools.

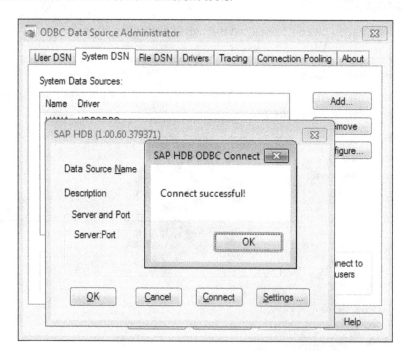

Let's configure SAP BO Explorer to connect to SAP HANA

Connection settings have to be maintained in **Central Management Console** (**CMC**) for SAP BO Explorer to connect to SAP HANA directly. By providing the details here, SAP BO Explorer connects to SAP HANA using JDBC.

Follow the given steps to connect to SAP BO Explorer:

1. Launch CMC in the browser and log in, as shown in the following screenshot. The URL format for CMC is `http://<server address>:8080/BOE/CMC`.

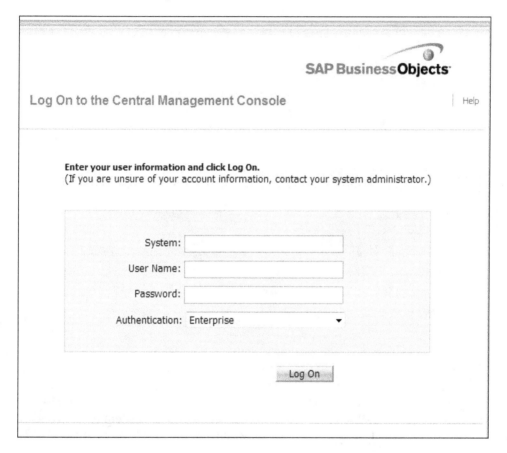

2. Go to **Applications** and open the settings for **Explorer**, as shown in the following screenshot:

3. In the pop-up window, maintain the required settings by providing the system name against `newdb.system.alias`, URL (IP address for the system) against `newdb.url`, and user ID and password against `newdb.user` and `newdb.password` respectively. Click on the **Save and Close** pop up. That's it! Now we can connect to SAP HANA from SAP BO Explorer without any intermediate layers, as shown in the following screenshot. We can now access analytic views and calculation views.

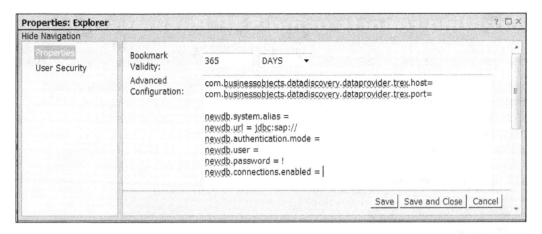

How it works...

To consume data in SAP HANA, JDBC and ODBC are the two most popular ways.
These connections are used by the reporting tools. Universes can also be built by
using a JDBC/ODBC connection in **Information Design Tool** (**IDT**). We use a universe
as a semantic layer to access data from SAP HANA for the SAP BO tools, that is,
Web Intelligence (WebI) and SAP BO Dashboards. SAP BO Explorer and SAP Crystal
Reports can access data from SAP HANA using universes and also directly from SAP
HANA using the JDBC/ODBC connection.

There's more...

The ODBC configuration that we set up in **Control Panel** can be used in IDT to create a
universe on top of SAP HANA using ODBC connectivity.

See also

> ▶ Videos on how to use different reporting tools are available at http://scn.sap.
> com/docs/DOC-34403

Creating reports using SAP BusinessObjects Web Intelligence

SAP BusinessObjects Web Intelligence (SAP BO WebI) is part of the **SAP BusinessObjects Platform** (**SBOP**) client tools family. When the SBOP client tools are installed, we get SAP BO WebI. The unique feature of WebI is that it is an ad hoc reporting tool. It helps users to create/ modify their own queries for the report. WebI gives a detailed level of reports. Using WebI, we can display the results in tabular or graphical formats. When we have a requirement to analyze data in a detailed fashion, we go with SAP WebI. This recipe explains how to create WebI documents on top of SAP HANA.

Getting ready

There are different reporting tools that are part of SAP BusinessObjects. As mentioned earlier, usage of the tool depends on the user's requirement. As of now, only SAP BusinessObjects reporting tools are officially supported by SAP. For this to work, we need to install SAP BusinessObjects Platform (SBOP) 4.X Client Tools and the SAP BO server.

How to do it...

We will create a universe using IDT with the following steps:

1. Launch IDT by navigating to **Start Menu | SAP Business Intelligence | SAP BusinessObjects BI platform 4 Client Tools | Information Design Tool**, as shown in the following screenshot:

2. To create a universe, we need a project in IDT. Hence a project has to be created first.

   Navigate to **File | New | Project**, or click on 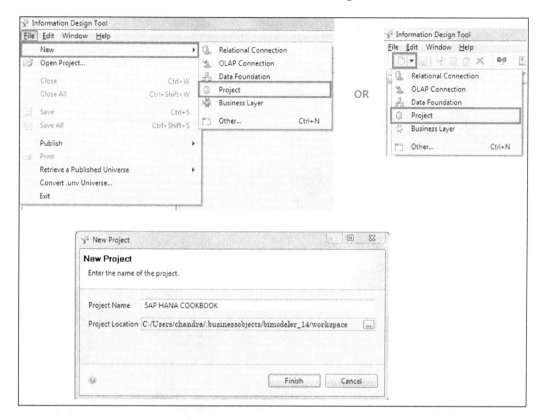 and select **Project**. Name the project and click on **Finish**, as shown in the following screenshot:

3. From the context menu of the project created, select **New | Relational Connection**. Name the connection. In the next screen, a list of drivers will be displayed. From the list, navigate to **SAP | SAP HANA database 1.0 | JDBC/ODBC drivers** and click on **Next**. Provide login credentials of the SAP HANA user ID and click on **Test Connection** to verify the connection status to SAP HANA. A pop up appears to tell us whether the connection is met with success or failure. In the next screen, we can set different parameters for the connection. After setting parameters, a connection will be created.

   A universe can be created using any connection. For ODBC connectivity, the system uses an ODBC configuration, which was discussed in the previous recipe.

The connection created in this step will be non-secure, as this is not published to a repository and is still a local object. The extension of the universe created will be .CNX.

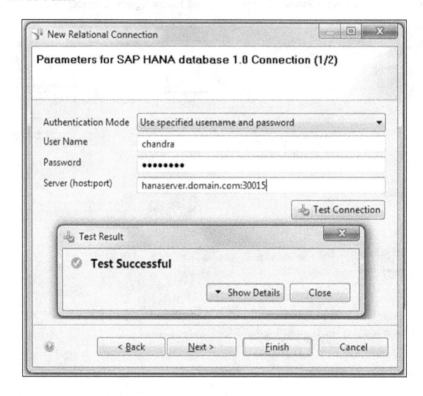

4. The created connection has to be published to the repository as publishing the connections makes it secure. While creating the business layer, we have to select the connection that has been published in this step. Only then can the created business layer be published to the repository to get access to the SAP BO tools. Publishing a connection to a repository can be done in four simple steps as follows:

   1. Right-click on the connection created (. CNX extension) and select **Publish Connection to a Repository**.

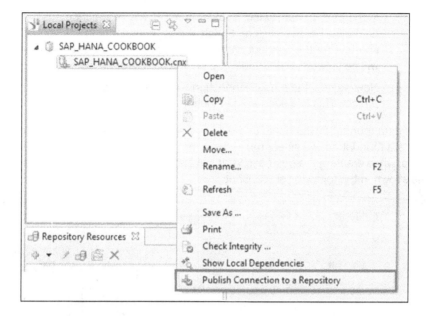

2. Provide the BO server login details and click on **Connect**.

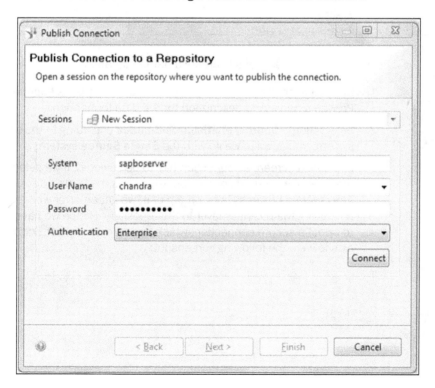

3. In the next screen, select a folder in which the connection has to be stored on the server and click on **Finish**. A pop up appears to ask you whether a shortcut for the connection has to be created. Select **Yes** so that a shortcut will be created in IDT under the project.

4. Now we can see a new connection with the .CNS extension under the project. This is a secured connection.

5. The data foundation connects to the source system, SAP HANA in this case. In data foundation, we select tables from the SAP HANA system. In the next step, while creating the business layer, we choose the **Data Foundation** layer, as shown in the following screenshot:

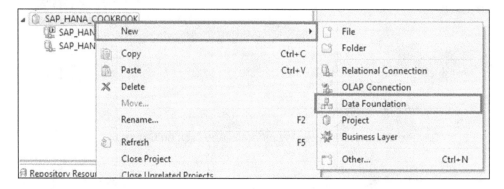

Now, follow the given steps to create a data foundation:

1. Right-click on the project folder and select **New | Data Foundation**. Provide a name and description for the data foundation.

2. Select **Single Source/Multisource-Enabled** according to the source system. In this case, we go with the **Single Source** system.

3. In the next screen, a connection has to be selected. If we select the local non-secured connection, which has the .CNX extension and create a business layer on top of it, we get an error while publishing the business layer to the repository. Hence we have to select a secure connection, which has an extension of .CNS, as shown in the following screenshot:

4. This creates a data foundation `.DFX` file under the project. Using the
    connection we used to create a data foundation, it gets connected
    to SAP HANA and displays all the available tables and column views.
    We know that information views (attribute, analytic, and calculation
    views) are stored as column views under the `_SYS_BIC` schema.
    Hence, to create reports on top of the information view, `_SYS_BIC` has
    to be expanded and the corresponding column view has to be searched
    for, as shown in the following screenshot:

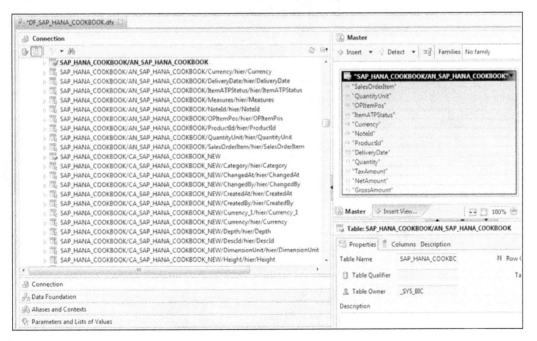

5. After selecting the required tables, save the data foundation.

After the data foundation is ready, we need a business layer. A business layer is created on top of the data foundation that is created in the previous step. A business layer is just to implement business terminologies for fields, such as changing technical names present in SAP HANA to the business field names, which gives more meaning to the end users. To create a business layer, follow the given steps:

1. From the context menu of the project, select **New | Business Layer**, as shown in the following screenshot:

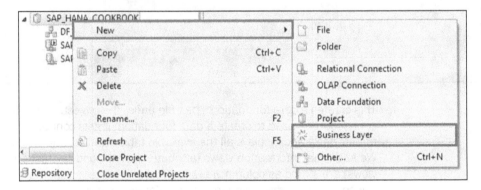

2. Now select **Relational Data Foundation** or **OLAP Connection**, as shown in the following screenshot. As we have selected JDBC while creating the data foundation, **Relational Data Foundation** has to be selected in this case.

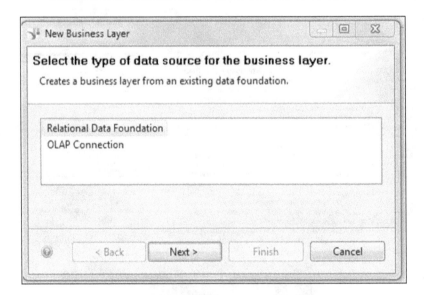

3. Give a name and add a description for the business layer.

4. Select **Data Foundation** from the list. All the data foundations available in this project will be listed here, as shown in the following screenshot:

5. A folder will be created with all the objects, as shown in the following screenshot. The objects that have to act as measures are to be changed to measures manually.

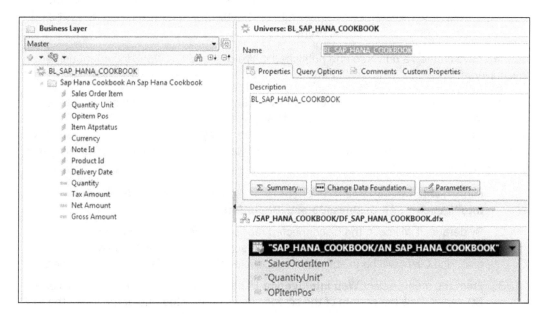

6. Save the business layer and from the **Project** menu, navigate to the context menu of the business layer and select **Publish | To a Repository**. As mentioned earlier, if a data foundation is created using a local connection (non-secured), an error will be thrown while publishing the business layer, as shown in the following screenshot:

7. After publishing the business layer into the required folder in the server, a universe will be created with an extension of . UNX. This can be accessed from any SAP BO reporting tool.

Now, we have created a universe and published it. We can create a WebI document using this universe.

To create reports using Web Intelligence, a universe should be readily available, which we have already created. Reports can be created using Web Intelligence Rich Client, which comes as part of SBOP Client Tools. They can also be created using BI Launch Pad, which is an URL, and can be executed in a browser. To do this, we will look at the creation of reports using Rich Client, as follows:

1. Launch **Web Intelligence Rich Client** by navigating to **Start | SAP Business Intelligence | SAP BusinessObjects BI platform 4 Client Tools**.

2. By default, it will be in the disconnected mode. We can check whether we are connected or not on the bottom right of the screen. The status will be displayed and also Rich Client will be in standalone mode, which can be seen at the top of the tool.

3. From the menu, select **Web Intelligence | Login as**. Give the login credentials of the BO server. Now the bottom of the screen shows **Connected** and at the top of the tool, we can see the connection to the server is successful.

4. Click on **Universe** or from the menu bar, select ⬜ followed by ⚹ Universe
   Select a universe as a data source. .

5. All the universes published to the repository will be displayed. Browse for our universe or search for it by its name and select the universe.

6. All the objects along with the folder will be displayed. Drag the required fields into the **Result Objects** pane and click on **Run Query**, as shown in the following screenshot.

7. A document with a table will be created. Save the document. By default, the report will be saved in **Personal Analysis** and can be viewed again only by the user who created it. Saving this in the server under the public folder makes it available for all the users.

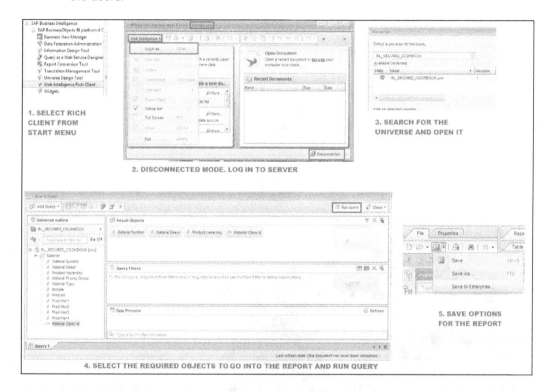

8. When this report is saved in the BO Server Public folder, we can open this from BI Launch Pad. The URL for BI Launch Pad will be similar to the URL for CMC, except that CMC will be replaced with BI in the URL, that is, the URL will be as shown:

```
http://<server address>:8080/BOE/BI
```

9. Log in to **BI launch pad** and go to the **Documents** tab. Select **Folders** from the bottom left of the screen and browse to the folder where we saved the Webl document, as shown in the following screenshot. We will see the list of reports available and their types, that is, Webl/Explorer/Crystal Reports, and so on.

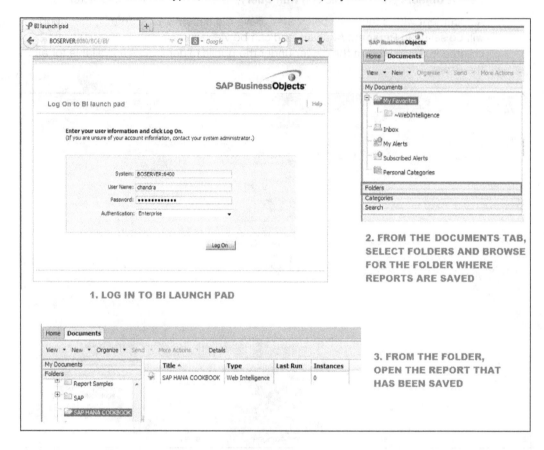

These are the steps involved in creating Webl documents (using Webl Rich Client) on top of SAP HANA.

How it works...

SAP BusinessObjects Platform consists of a set of client tools. This includes Webl Rich Client to create Webl documents, IDT to create universes, which act as semantic layers on top of SAP HANA, **Query as a Web Service** (**QAWS**) designer to create customized web services for specific queries, and so on. In this section, we will cover how to create reports using Webl on top of SAP HANA. To create Webl reports, we need a universe to access data from SAP HANA.

As stated, a universe acts as a semantic layer and is created using IDT. This creates a layer in between SAP HANA and the SAP BO tools, and the data is passed through this layer. No data is staged in the universe. Once the universe is ready, we can create the WebI report using the published universe. Connectivity to SAP HANA, that is, JDBC/ODBC depends on the connection we use while creating a universe in IDT. Let us start by creating a universe using IDT and the WebI document on top of it.

There's more...

We can create WebI reports from BI Launch Pad also. Log in to **BI launch pad** and select [icon], and then click on **Select a Universe as a source**, as shown in the following screenshot. The next steps will be similar to the steps we followed to create the WebI report from Rich Client.

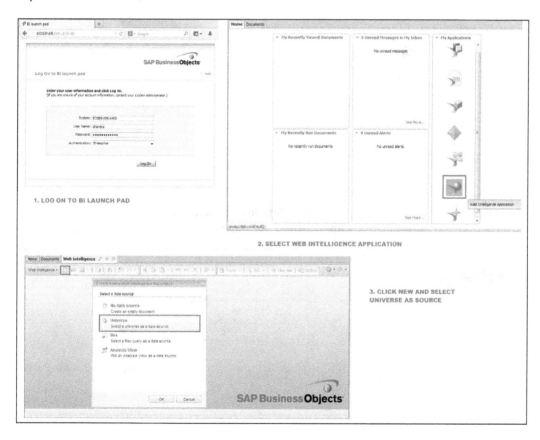

The process is almost the same as how we create reports using WebI Rich Client. Log on to **BI launch pad** by opening it in a web browser, as shown in the following screenshot:

After logging on to BI Launch Pad, open **Web Intelligence Application** from the **Applications** menu or from the icons under **My Applications**, as shown in the following screenshot:

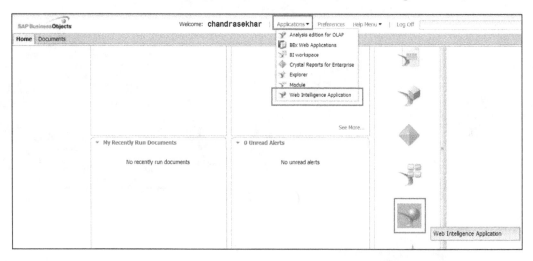

A new tab with the WebI application will be launched. Now, click on **New** (*Ctrl + N*). A pop-up window will be opened to select a data source. Select **Universe** as the data source and click on **OK**, as shown in the following screenshot. The next steps will be the same as creating a WebI report using WebI Rich Client.

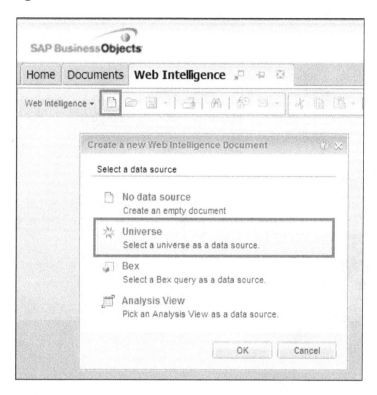

See also

▸ More information on WebI, the best practices to use WebI on top of SAP HANA, and FAQs can be found at the following links:

- ❑ http://wiki.sdn.sap.com/wiki/display/BBA/
  BI+Tools+and+the+BI+Platform

- ❑ http://scn.sap.com/docs/DOC-30614

- ❑ http://scn.sap.com/community/businessobjects-
  web-intelligence/blog/2012/07/23/faq--sap-bi4-
  webintelligence-on-hana

Creating reports using SAP BusinessObjects Explorer

In this recipe, we will see how to create SAP BO Explorer Information Space on top of SAP HANA information views.

Getting ready

Separate client tools are available to install SAP BO Explorer. We can also launch this from BI Launch Pad. So, we just need SAP BI Launch Pad credentials and authorizations to create Information Spaces in Explorer.

How to do it...

To create an Information Space in SAP BO Explorer, we have to log in to BI Launch Pad and navigate to **Explorer**. Then, we have to create the spaces and save them. We require to follow the given steps:

1. Log in to **BI launch pad** and select **Explorer** from the bottom of the list, as shown in the following screenshot:

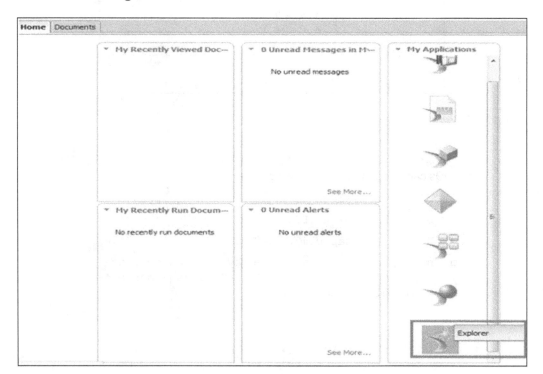

2. On the **Home** screen, we can see all the Information Spaces created. Now, click on **Manage Spaces** on the top of the screen. We can select the analytic view from the system directly using the parameters maintained from CMC or by using the connection created in IDT. In this case, we will use the connection created and published in IDT. Browse to the analytic view using the connection created in IDT (**SAP_HANA_COOKBOOK**). All the spaces created on this analytic view will be displayed on the right-hand side of the screen. We will create an Information Space on the **SAP_HANA_COOKBOOK** analytical view. For this to happen, click on New.

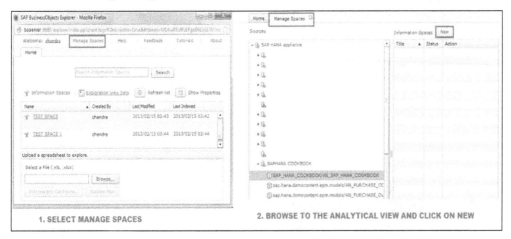

| 1. SELECT MANAGE SPACES | 2. BROWSE TO THE ANALYTICAL VIEW AND CLICK ON NEW |

3. In the next window when creating an **Information Space**, under the **Objects** tab, **Name** is a mandatory field. Give a name and description to the Information Space and move to the next tab, **Objects**. In this tab, add all the required objects and attributes/measures. We can rename the attributes or measures, or create a new calculated measure. Click on **OK** after adding the objects, as shown in the following screenshot:

4. In the **Manage Spaces** tab, against the analytic view, an Information Space will be created. **Status** will be blank and under **Action,** we will see **Index Now**. After creating or modifying objects in **Information Spaces**, indexing is required so that the data gets indexed. Click on **Index Now**. After the completion of indexing, we can see the status with a green arrow mark 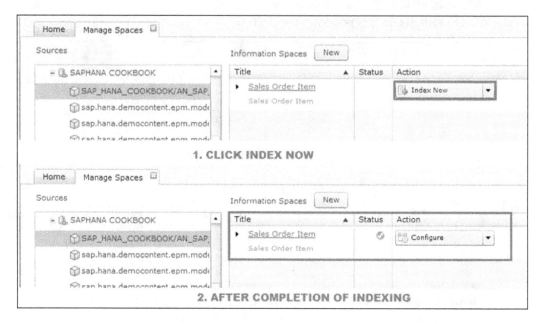 and under **Action**, click on **Configure**. With this step, the Information Space is created, as shown in the following screenshot:

5. Under the **Home** tab, we can find the Information Space created. Click on that to open it and we can explore the data. There will be different options, such as to share, change the mode of displaying results, and so on. The number of records and the data retrieval time will be displayed on the right-hand side of the screen, as shown in the following screenshot:

How it works...

SAP BO Explorer connects to SAP HANA directly using the connection parameters we set in CMC. A universe is not mandatory to start creating reports in SAP BO Explorer on top of SAP HANA. Explorer is used to get answers on-the-fly for the questions we ask. It is a kind of a Q & A tool, where results are displayed for the questions we pose to Explorer. It uses the search mechanism of pre-indexed data. As Explorer directly connects to SAP HANA, results will be obtained in a very short time. Slicing and dicing data is possible instantly and relevant data can be managed based on the filters we apply. Tabular and graphical modes of display are possible. We can also export the results to CSV files or as an image. The results can also be shared with others through e-mail. Moreover, the report can be saved as a bookmark.

There's more...

The Information Space we created will be saved in the **Favorites** folder by default, as shown in the following screenshot. This can be saved in **Public Folders** in BI Launch Pad for access by users. To achieve this, select the corresponding folder while creating the Information Space.

The Information Space created can also be saved as **View Set** in **Public Folder** of BI Launch Pad. Follow the given steps:

1. Select **Create View Set**.

2. Give a name for the view set. Visual elements can be modified by dragging them to the main screen area.

3. Click on **Save as.** This will open a new pop up asking for **Name** and **Description**, as shown in the following screenshot:

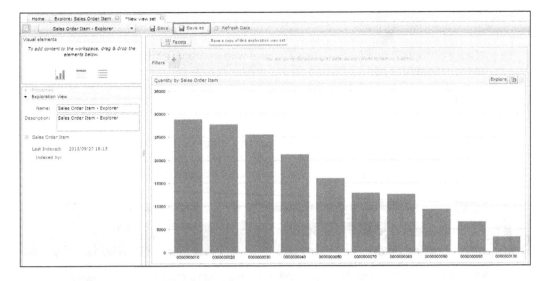

4. Provide a name and description for the view set. Select a folder where this has to be saved, as shown in the following screenshot:

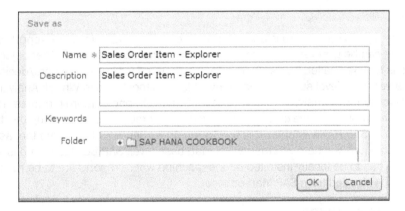

5. Now, we can see the view set saved in the public folder that we have selected, as shown in the following screenshot:

See also

▶ More information on SAP Business Explorer with interactive videos is available at the following links:

- ❑ http://www.saphana.com/community/learn/solutions/explorer

- ❑ http://scn.sap.com/docs/DOC-8675

- ❑ http://scn.sap.com/community/sap-runs-sap/
  blog/2013/04/16/how-sap-runs-hana-analytics-in-business-
  objects-explorer-for-several-thousand-users

Creating reports using SAP BusinessObjects Dashboards/Xcelsius

Dashboard is a visualization tool. In this recipe, we are going to create a simple dashboard report on top of SAP HANA.

Getting ready

SAP BusinessObjects Dashboard is a visualization tool. This is an interactive reporting tool where reports can be generated in the form of graphs, charts, maps, and other objects. Originally this tool was called **Xcelsius**. This tool is intended for business users/decision makers at a very high level such as measuring KPIs. This tool helps in What-If Analysis of the data, which helps in analyzing different sets of values in one or more formulae. The only limitation of this tool is that we cannot handle very large amounts of data using this tool. But the power of SAP HANA enables this tool to run on a huge amount of data too, as the analysis/calculations will be performed at the database level. SAP BO Dashboard is a client tool; hence, it has to be locally installed on the machine where reports are to be run from. This can be downloaded from SAP Marketplace.

How to do it...

Now we will see how to acquire data from SAP HANA for SAP BO Dashboard using the universe created in IDT. Follow the given steps:

1. After installing SAP BO Dashboard, launch it from the **Start** menu by navigating to the **SAP Business Intelligence | SAP BusinessObjects Dashboards 4** folder.

2. Open a new blank model.

3. From the pane on the left-hand side of the model, select **Query Browser**, then click on **Add Query** and log in to the SAP BO server, as shown in the following screenshot:

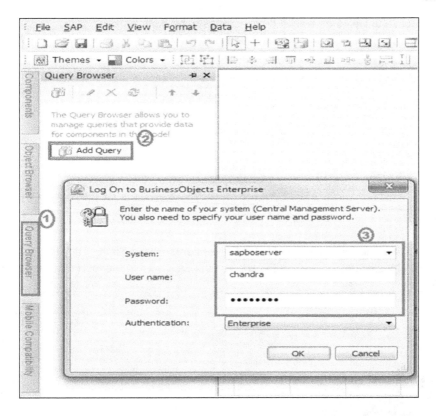

4. We can see the available types of data sources: **Universe** and **BEx**. Select **Universe** as the source, as we will create the report on top of the universe that we built earlier, and click on **Next**, as shown in the following screenshot:

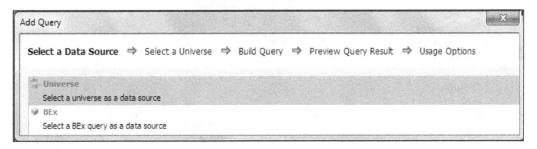

5. Select a universe on which the report has to be built. Here, we select **BL_SECURED_COOKBOOK**, as shown in the following screenshot:

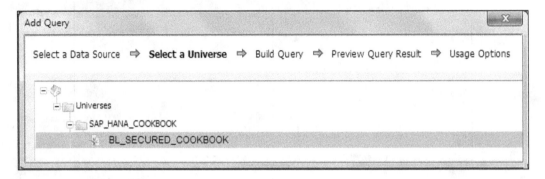

6. Add the required fields into **Result Objects** and click on **Next**. If any filters are required, we can add to the **Filters** section, as shown in the following screenshot:

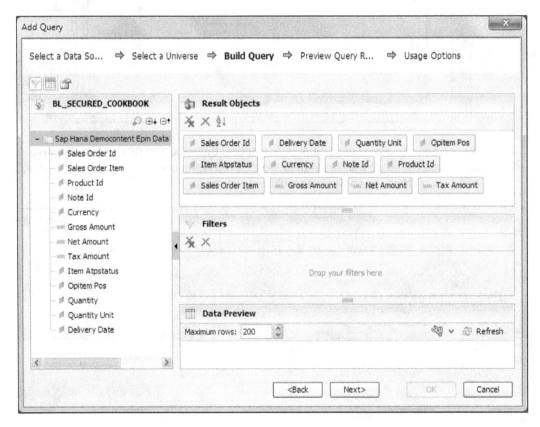

7. Now, we will see the data preview of the query we have selected. Click on **OK**, as shown in the following screenshot:

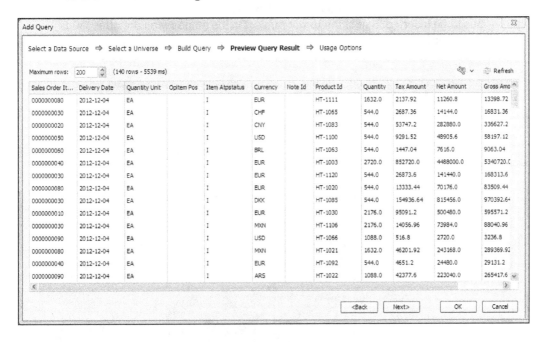

8. Insert data from the query into the spreadsheet. Select each field in the **Query Browser** pane and click on the icon just beneath **Insert in Spreadsheet**, as shown in the following screenshot. A pop-up window will open to select a range where the data has to be inserted. Select the target range. Do the same for all the other fields which are required for reporting.

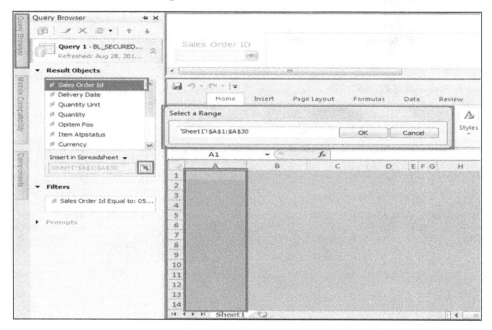

9. Insert a column chart and assign **Sales Order ID**, **Gross Amount**, **Net Amount**, and **Tax Amount** into rows and columns accordingly, as shown in the following screenshot:

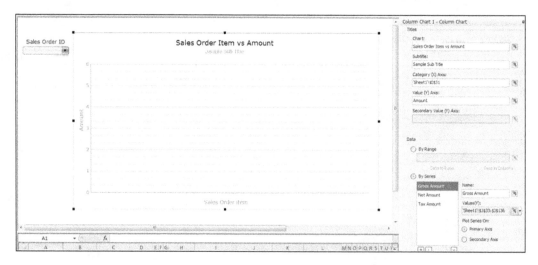

10. Preview the data. We can see the output, as shown in the following screenshot:

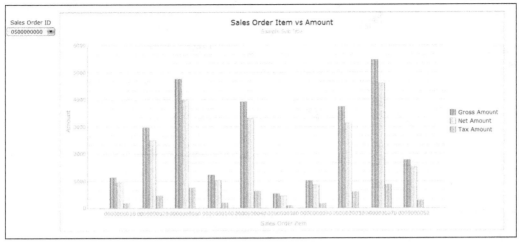

11. This result can be exported into any format as required, and shared, similar to the process we followed for SAP BO Dashboards.

How it works...

Dashboard is an excellent visualization tool for summarized data. From SAP BO Dashboard SP5, we can connect to the universe created in IDT on top of SAP HANA. This is not available in the previous versions of the Dashboard. IDT connects to SAP HANA using JDBC/ODBC connections and the universe is built as described in the previous recipes of the chapter. The universe created in IDT works as an intermediary layer between SAP HANA and SAP BO Dashboard. On top of this, we can access the universe and create a query in SAP BO Dashboard, with an option of filters too. With these capabilities, SAP BO Dashboard will overcome the limitations in terms of the volume of data that it can handle.

See also

▶ Another example of how to create a dashboard on top of SAP HANA can be found at http://scn.sap.com/docs/DOC-43919

Creating reports using SAP BusinessObjects Analysis for OLAP

SAP BO Analysis for OLAP has been introduced as part of the SAP BO family from SAP BusinessObjects BI4.X Version. This has enabled multidimensional reporting in SAP BO, through which we can access SAP BW queries, cubes, and so on. This helps users to take a decision on multidimensional data. This is a web-based interface that can be launched from SAP BI Launch Pad. Hence, no separate installation is required on local client machines.

How to do it...

Let's create an OLAP connection in CMC for SAP HANA.

An OLAP connection is mandatory to connect SAP BO Office Analysis for OLAP to SAP HANA. The connection has to be created in CMC. Follow the given steps:

1. Log on to CMC and select **OLAP Connections**. Then, go to the corresponding folder and select the **New connection** icon from the toolbar, as shown in the following screenshot:

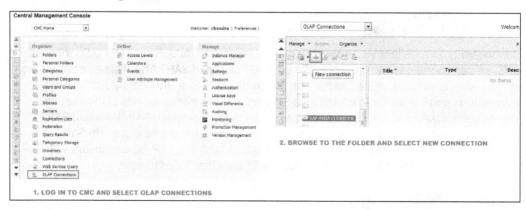

2. Provide **a name** for the connection, **a description**, and server details, and then click on **Connect**. A pop-up window appears asking for login credentials. Enter the SAP HANA credentials. Now all the analytic and calculation views (in the form of cubes) in the SAP HANA system will be displayed. Select the cube and click on **Select**. Now this will include the package as **InfoProvider** and the analytic view as **Query**. Click on **Save**. This will create a connection in the folder we selected with the analytic view as **Query**, as shown in the following screenshot:

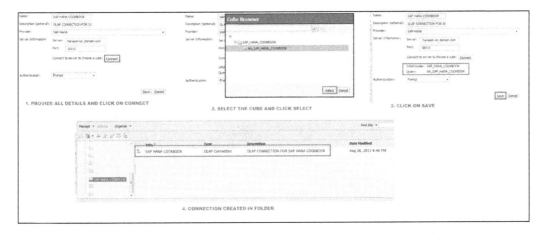

Let's create a workspace in the SAP BO Analysis edition for OLAP:

1. Log in to SAP BI Launch Pad and select **Analysis edition for OLAP** from the **My Applications** menu, as shown in the following screenshot:

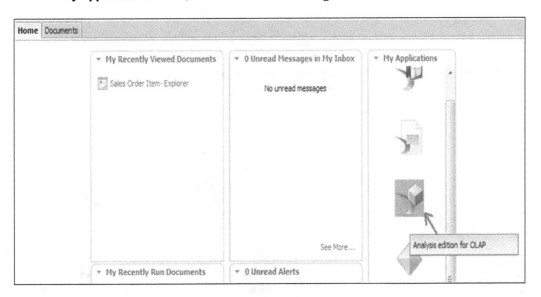

2. From the list of available cubes, select the one that has been created in CMC. Select **SAP HANA COOKBOOK** in this case. Then provide the SAP HANA system credentials.

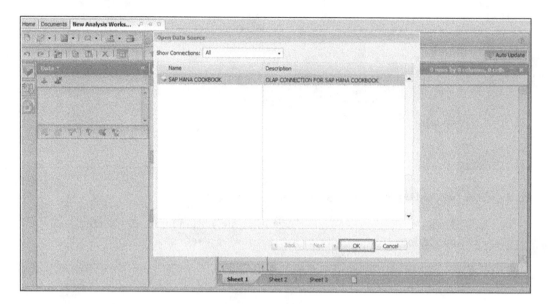

3. Drag-and-drop attributes and measures into rows and columns to obtain the data, as shown in the following screenshot:

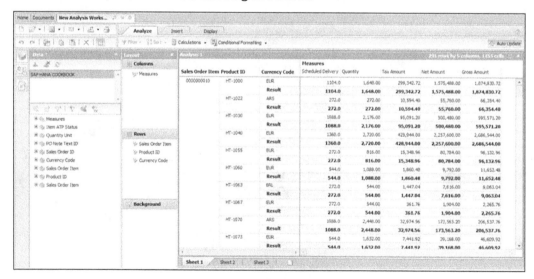

4. Save the analysis in the public folder, so that it can be accessed by all the users, as shown in the following screenshot:

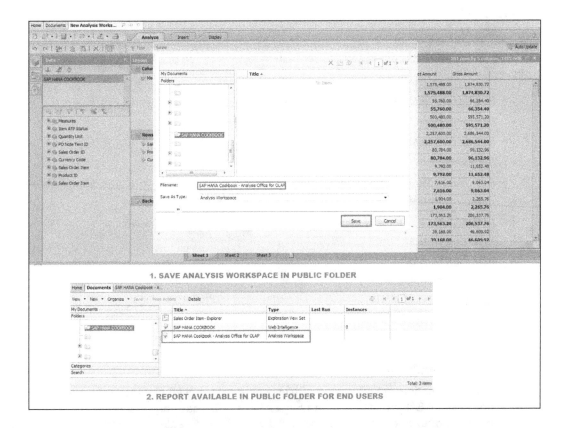

1. SAVE ANALYSIS WORKSPACE IN PUBLIC FOLDER

2. REPORT AVAILABLE IN PUBLIC FOLDER FOR END USERS

How it works...

The OLAP tool is very helpful when we have a data set with more dimensions and comparatively less measures for analysis. In this case, it is very difficult to slice and dice the data set. OLAP functionality makes this possible with minimum performance in reports execution as data is precalculated in the cubes. This tool is mainly intended for a very small set of people, who are business analysts. This is because all the users may not be able make the right decision by maintaining such a huge number of dimensions with less measures. Hence, adding the OLAP tool into the SAP BO family has helped many users to analyze multidimensional data using the OLAP functionality.

When compared to Webl, drill-down capabilities and speed will be much better in SAP BO Analysis for OLAP as data is precalculated at different levels of the cube. The analysis made using this tool can also be shared across different tools such as Webl and Explorer. To create reports using SAP BO Analysis for OLAP on top of SAP HANA, we should have an OLAP connection set up and use this while creating reports.

There's more...

Different workflows that SAP BO Analysis for OLAP supports on top of SAP HANA are as follows:

- ▸ Saving/opening a workbook to/from the Business Intelligence platform server
- ▸ Undo/redo
- ▸ Defining style sets for crosstabs
- ▸ Swapping axes
- ▸ Analyzing data with the design panel
- ▸ Filtering members
- ▸ Sorting data by members and measures
- ▸ Inserting charts
- ▸ Inserting filter components
- ▸ Converting crosstab cells to formulas
- ▸ Creating presentations
- ▸ Pause/refresh

See also

- ▸ More information on SAP BusinessObjects Analysis for OLAP and the best practices for SAP can be found at `http://www.sdn.sap.com/irj/scn/go/portal/prtroot/docs/library/uuid/b0c79848-2a24-3010-fc9c-f2f7448a75b3?overridelayout=true`

Creating reports using Microsoft Excel

Though many reporting tools are available on the market, many users still use MS Excel to report. In this section, we will cover analysis of data from SAP HANA in Excel.

Getting ready

Microsoft Excel can also be used to consume data from SAP HANA and act as a reporting tool for users. Excel is still used as a reporting tool in many parts of the BI world to access and analyze data.

How to do it...

Let's create a connection to SAP HANA. Follow the given steps:

1. From the **Data** tab, select **From Other Sources**. This will open a pop up with all the available OLE DB provider types. Scroll down and select **SAP HANA MDX Provider** from the list and then click on the **Next** button, as shown in the following screenshot:

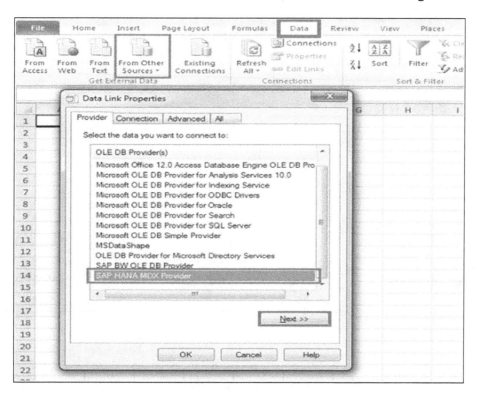

2. Now, provide all the login details of SAP HANA to create the connection. Click on **Test Connection**, as shown in the following screenshot. A pop-up window will come up with the status of testing the connection. Now click on the **OK** button.

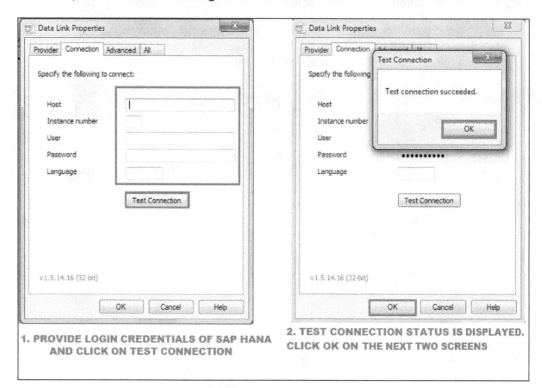

1. PROVIDE LOGIN CREDENTIALS OF SAP HANA AND CLICK ON TEST CONNECTION

2. TEST CONNECTION STATUS IS DISPLAYED. CLICK OK ON THE NEXT TWO SCREENS

3. From the dropdown, select the database. The database is the same as the package we have in the SAP HANA system. All the cubes, which are nothing but analytic views in SAP HANA in the package, are selected. Select a cube on which the report is to be generated and select **Next**. In the next screen, give a name to the analysis document and provide the description if required. Now, select **Pivot Table** from the pop up and click on **OK**.

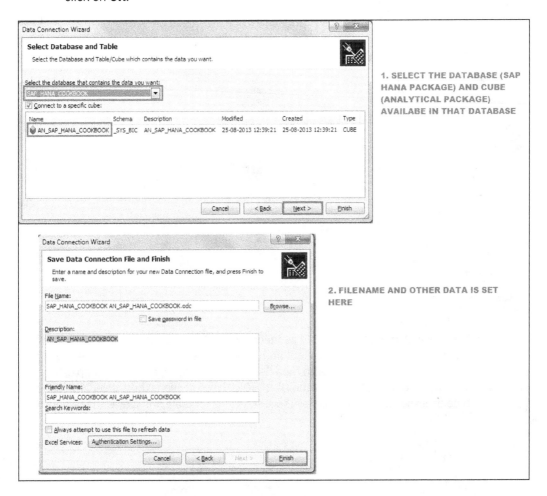

4. Now, a pivot table will be created. Select the fields on which analysis is to be done and play with the data, as shown in the following screenshot:

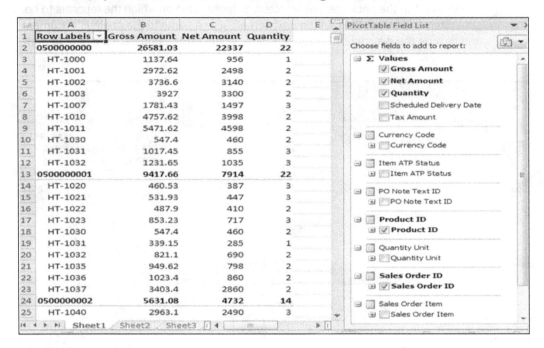

How it works...

Excel uses SAP HANA MDX Provider to build connections to SAP HANA, thereby giving us the results. The capability for Excel to access data from SAP HANA and display the results in a pivot table is an outstanding way to explore data from SAP HANA. The steps are pretty simple, that is, creating a connection to SAP HANA using the ODBO (OLAP) connection. Then, select the cube which has to be accessed and finally display the results in pivot table and play with the data.

There's more...

We can also connect to SAP HANA using ODBC drivers. When we connect using OLE DB drivers, the restriction is that we can access only the cubes (analytic views), but if we use the ODBC connectivity, we can access tables as well. Let us see how to connect to SAP HANA from Excel using the ODBC connectivity:

1. From the **Data** tab of Excel, select **From Other Sources** and then **From Microsoft Query**, as shown in the following screenshot:

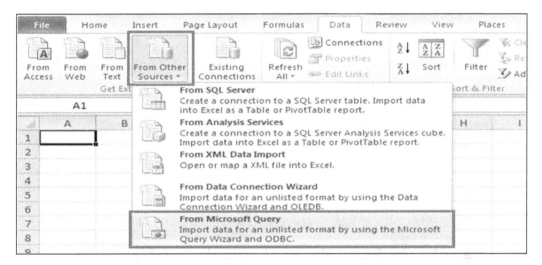

2. Select **<New Datasource>** and then give the name of the data source. From the drop-down menu, select the HANA-related ODBC driver, **HDBODBC32**. Click on **Connect** and provide the server details of SAP HANA and the login credentials, as shown in the following screenshot:

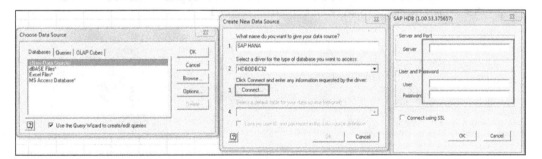

3. After successfully connecting to the SAP HANA system, we can access all the tables from schemas and information views from packages. Select the required table/view. In this case, we will select the **SAP_HANA_COOKBOOK** analytic view. Select the required columns into the output. In the next two screens, select filters and sorting based on the columns as required. Finally click on **Finish** to see the output in the Excel sheet, as shown in the following screenshot:

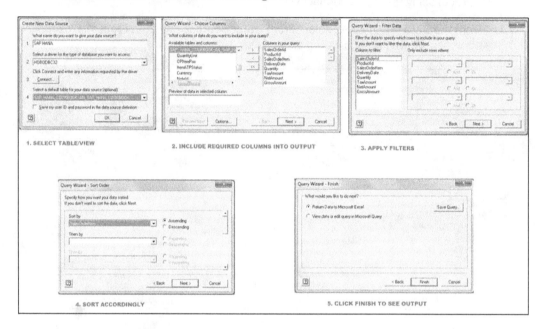

There is an excellent book that explains SAP HANA integration with Microsoft Excel by Packt Publishing, available at `http://www.packtpub.com/article/sap-hana integration-with-microsoft-excel`

See also

▶ There is an excellent book that explains SAP HANA integration with Microsoft Excel by Packt Publishing, available at `http://www.packtpub.com/article/sap-hana integration-with-microsoft-excel`

- More information on reporting in Excel on top of SAP HANA is available at the following links:

  - `http://scn.sap.com/community/developer-center/hana/`
    `blog/2013/07/19/how-to-setup-excel-2007-on-hana-sp05-`
    `with-windows-7-64bit`

  - `http://www.sdn.sap.com/irj/scn/go/portal/prtroot/docs/`
    `library/uuid/e03fef5e-d82f-2f10-8898-859c4ed57e62?quickl`
    `ink=index&overridelayout=true`

  - `http://www.saphana.com/docs/DOC-2376`

Creating reports in SAP Lumira

SAP Lumira is a powerful reporting tool for end users. Earlier, it was known as SAP Visual Intelligence. In this recipe, we will see how to create models in SAP Lumira on top of SAP HANA.

Getting ready

SAP Lumira is a self-service BI tool for data analysis. Formerly, it was known as SAP Visual Intelligence. We can also manipulate and transform data from different source systems. It is a standalone too that has to be installed on the client machine. SAP Lumira is targeted for end users or decision makers, so that they can access data from the source and create their own ad hoc models. Being a client-based tool, this has to be installed on the machine where it will be used. To create models in SAP Lumira, the user ID that we use to log into SAP HANA from SAP Lumira must have some privileges. The user ID must have the MODELING role. Also, the `_SYS_REPO` user must have the SELECT authorization on the schema, which we access from SAP Lumira. We can perform only `Max`, `Min`, `Count`, and `Sum` on measures in SAP HANA.

How to do it...

We can create models in SAP Lumira on top of information views or tables. The steps for creating Lumira models are as shown:

1. Launch SAP Lumira from the **Start** menu by navigating to the **SAP Business Intelligence | SAP Lumira** folder.

2. Click on **New Document** and select **SAP HANA One Online** as the source, as shown in the following screenshot.

The difference between the SAP HANA online and offline modes is that in the online mode, we cannot create any measures in SAP Lumira. All the measures will be detected from SAP HANA. Hence when we are using the online mode, if any objects are required for reporting, they have to be created at the SAP HANA end.

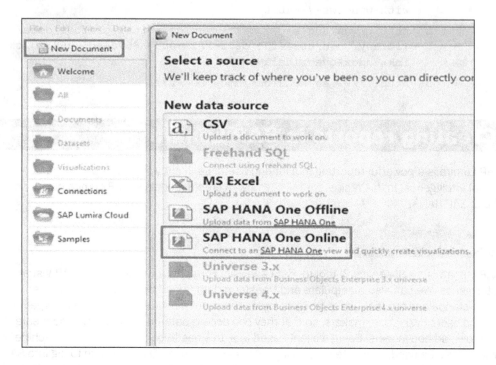

3. Provide details of the SAP HANA server and the login credentials to access tables/views from SAP HANA. Search for the required table/view and click on **Acquire**.

    The **Preview and select data** checkbox can be used to have a glance at the data before acquiring it, and to select only selective columns, as shown in the following screenshot:

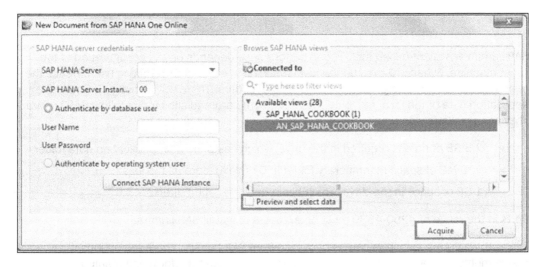

4. Now select the required attributes in the X axis and measures in the Y axis, as shown in the following screenshot. By default, the results will be in the column bar chart. We can change the visualization available here.

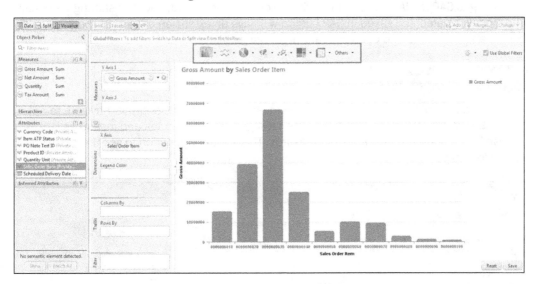

5. Click on the **Share** button on the top to share the result set.

How it works...

SAP Lumira is a client-based tool, whose performance depends on the configuration of the client machine. **Sybase IQ** runs on the local machine in which SAP Lumira is used. Hence the system requires high configuration to support SAP Lumira. There will be two `.iq` files in the application data of the local machine. There are some prerequisites for installing SAP Lumira. They are as follows with respect to drive space:

- 2.5 GB of data is required in the drive, which hosts the user application data folder
- 200 MB of space in temporary folder in C drive to store all the logs
- 1 GB of space in the drive, which hosts the installation directory

Ports in the range of 4250-4539 must be available to install SAP Lumira.

Tables and information views can be accessed from SAP Lumira. There are options to merge multiple data sources. On this acquired data, we can transform and manipulate data before saving the model or sharing with the users. SAP Lumira supports different types of visualizations, such as bar charts, line charts, pie charts, geographic analysis, bubble charts, heat map, waterfall map, and so on. The resulting sets can be shared in the form of a file, publishing to SAP HANA, SAP StreamWork, Explorer, Lumira Cloud, and also sharing via e-mail. The models created and saved in SAP Lumira will have an extension of `.svid`. These models can be also be shared and opened in any other SAP Lumira tool.

There's more...

After a model is built; if we want to remove some columns from the analysis, navigate to **Data | Edit Source**. Now in a new window, we will get all the attributes and measures. We can include only few attributes or measures. There is also an option to see the sample values for attributes.

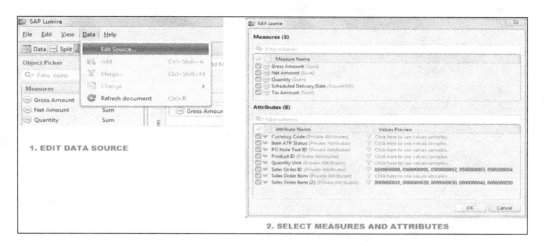

See also

▸ SAP Lumira user guide, new features of SAP Lumira, and an example of data consumption from SAP HANA are available at the following links:

- ❏ `http://scn.sap.com/community/lumira/blog/2013/06/13/reviewing-sap-lumira-new-features-clarissa-explains-it-all`
- ❏ `http://help.sap.com/businessobject/product_guides/vi01/en/vi1_0_11_user_en.pdf`
- ❏ `http://scn.sap.com/community/developer-center/hana/blog/2013/07/19/building-an-analytic-calculation-view-from-the-hana-tables-for-use-with-sap-lumira`

5
Advanced Features in SAP HANA

In this chapter, we will cover:

- ► Converting different currencies
- ► Creating hierarchies
- ► Creating variables
- ► Creating input parameters
- ► Creating filters
- ► Creating procedures using SQLScript
- ► Creating decision tables

Introduction

This chapter deals with advanced concepts such as creating hierarchies, stored procedures, variables, filters, and decision tables. These objects are not mandatory and are created only when really required. For example, we do a currency conversion when data comes in different currencies and reports are to be generated in a single currency.

Converting different currencies

In general, the businesses at any scale are geography-centric and based on the local currency. They are scattered across regions and continents. There is a strong significance to have the proper design and feature of currency conversion mechanism to ensure a robust, foolproof, and interconnected system in the database to calculate the key metrics or measures to ensure the numbers are correct. Posting orders, purchases, or invoicing is done in the local currency of where the sale happens. Business users or transaction specialists who execute the reports may be in the same or a different geographical region. For this reason, tables in SAP ERP, or any ERP for that matter, will have mandatory fields and an explicit nexus between the amount fields and the currencies. In this recipe, we will look at how to perform currency conversion.

How to do it...

The key stake objects or parameters are the source currency, target currency, and the impacted tables where the conversion rates are maintained before applying a currency conversion formula or technique. These tables must be imported to the schema, which is used in currency conversion. It is recommended to perform currency conversion in analytic views as the dimension objects or hierarchies can be utilized from the attribute views.

To start with currency conversion in SAP HANA, follow the given steps:

1. In the analytic view, select the measure (from the **Output** section) that the currency conversion has to be enabled for.

2. From the **Properties** pane, change the **Measure Type** to **Amount with Currency**, as shown in the following screenshot. This will be **Simple** by default.

3. Select the **Enable for conversion** checkbox and in the **Currency** dialog, select type: **Fixed** or **Column**. When we select **Fixed**, the currency will be selected from the TCURC table. If we select the type as **Column** and mention a specific column, values from that attribute in the view will be considered for conversion.

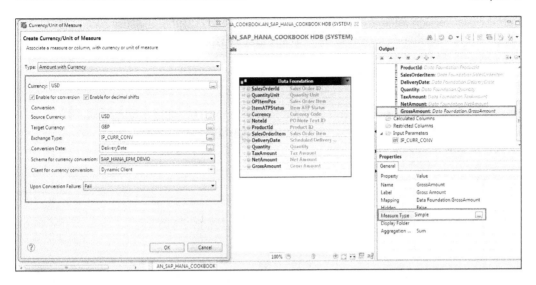

4. Provide **Source Currency** and **Target Currency**.

5. **Exchange Type** can be fixed (static) or an input parameter (dynamic). When the type is **Fixed**, the exchange type will be taken from the TCURW table. We can make this type a dynamic one that the user can select at runtime. This can be done using the input parameter.

6. Select **Conversion Date**. If this is fixed, the conversion date will be taken from the calendar. In the case of columns, this comes from the attribute used in the view. When this is an input parameter, the date can be taken at runtime from the user.

7. **Schema for currency conversion** should be the same schema that holds all the replicated currency tables.

How it works...

Metrics or measures in SAP HANA have their own type. By default, all the measures don't have a type, that is, unit of measure or currency. This makes a difference when compared to data in the SAP ERP tables. Hence, it is mandatory that conversions have to be explicitly maintained and applied to measures according to the reporting requirements for report consumers. Currency conversion arises mainly for scenarios such as global consolidation, statutory and legal obligation, and reporting. For example, consider Packt Publishing, one of the leading publishers, who publishes books across the globe. Invoices are made in different currencies to support the transaction locally, based on the region where the sales are made, whereas the global manager in the head office wants to see the results in British Pounds. To meet these requirements, currencies have to be converted into a global currency—in this case, the British Pound—before reports are generated. In scenarios such as these, currency conversion plays a significant role.

Currency conversion rates are usually maintained in the SAP ERP or ERP transactional tables: TCURR (exchange rates), TCURV (exchange rate types), TCURF (conversion factors), TCURN (quotations), and TCURX (currency decimal settings). These tables have to be replicated in SAP HANA and in the same schema that is used for the creation of views for report consumption.

When currency conversion is enabled for measures during calculations, the conversion rates are taken from the currency tables, and values are calculated on the fly. The values that are calculated are then displayed in reports.

See also

▶ More information on currency conversion and SAP tables that are related to exchange rates is available at the following links:

❏ http://scn.sap.com/community/hana-in-memory/
blog/2012/04/27/how-to-perform-currency-conversion-in-
sap-hana

❏ http://www.tcodesearch.com/sap-tables/
search?q=exchange+rate

Creating hierarchies

Hierarchies are created to maintain data in a structured format, such as maintaining customer or employee data based on their roles and splitting data based on geographies. Hierarchical data is very useful for organizational purposes during decision making.

How to do it...

Two types of hierarchies can be created in SAP HANA: the level hierarchy and parent-child hierarchy in the attribute view or analytic view. The hierarchies are initially created in the attribute view and later can be combined in the analytic view or calculation view for consumption in report as per business requirements. Let us create both types of hierarchies in attribute views. When these attribute views are used in analytic views, the hierarchies created in attribute views will be inherited to drill up, drill down, or drill across in the reports for multidimensional analysis.

Level hierarchy

Follow the given steps to create a level hierarchy:

1. In the attribute view, go to the **Semantics** section. On the hierarchies part of the screen, we can create or edit hierarchies. Click on **Create** (plus sign in the right corner of the screen), as shown in the following screenshot:

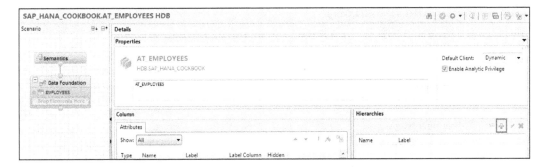

2. Give the name of the hierarchy and select the type as **Level Hierarchy** from the drop-down menu, as shown in the following screenshot:

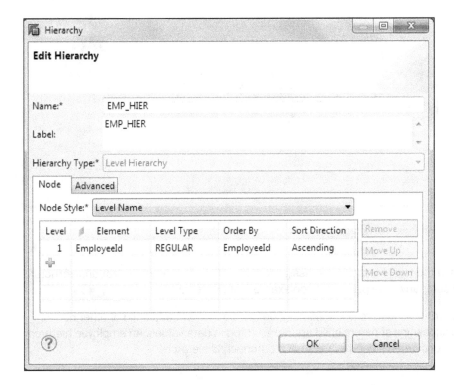

3. Include hierarchy fields, that is, the elements for different levels of the hierarchy.

The parent-child hierarchy

The steps are the same as creating a leveled hierarchy, except that we change the hierarchy type to **Parent-Child Hierarchy** and mention which field acts as the parent and which acts as the child.

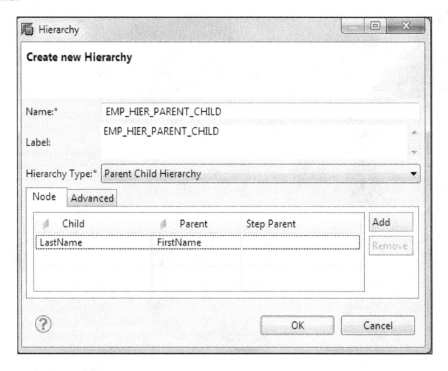

How it works...

Nodes in the level hierarchy are assigned a specific place. An organizational structure with a company code plan is a good example of a level hierarchy.

In a parent-child hierarchy, the same node can be a parent and child of other nodes. The relationships of parent-child are represented in data values. An employee hierarchy can be considered a good example of a parent-child hierarchy.

▶ Another example of hierarchy creation and a video are available at the following links:

❑ http://www.sapanalyticsguru.com/index.php/sap-hana/50-sap-hana-e-learning-hierarchies-and-calculated-columns-in-attribute-view

❑ http://scn.sap.com/docs/DOC-27466

Creating variables

Variables are used when values are to be determined dynamically. Variables can be created in analytic and calculation views on any field in the output definition of the view.

Getting ready

In order to create variables, we should have analytic or calculation views on hand. Having created one of these models, let us start creating variables.

How to do it...

In this recipe, we will see how to create variables in SAP HANA that enable end users to change values dynamically at the time of executing reports. Follow the given steps:

1. Open an analytic or calculation view and click on the **Semantics** section.

2. Under **Variables/Input Parameters**, click on the plus sign in the right corner of the screen and select **Create Variable**, as shown in the following screenshot:

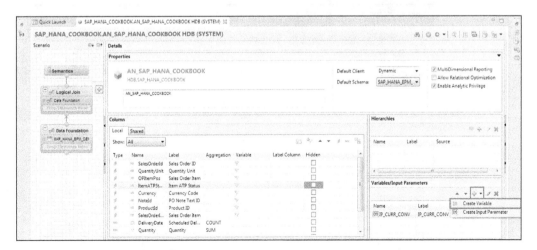

3. Enter information in all the fields and click on **OK**. The **Default Value** field is optional.

4. After creating a variable, we can see the variable against the field we selected in the **Semantics** section, as shown in the following screenshot:

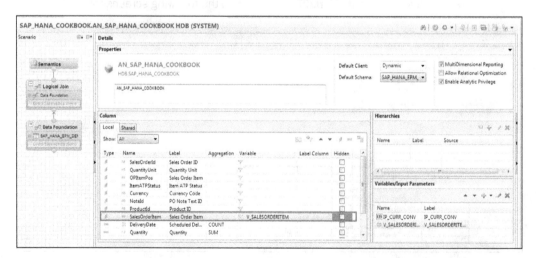

How it works...

Variables are tied to attributes and they hit the database along with the query in the WHERE clause. Variables are inherited to the next level if the views holding the variables are used. For example, if a variable is created in analytic views and these are used in calculation views, the variables will be available in the calculation view. But these variables cannot be edited in the calculation view. The variable has to be edited only in the analytic view where it is created.

See also

> ▶ Learn more about using SAP HANA variables and parameters in SAP BusinessObjects BI4.0 at http://scn.sap.com/docs/DOC-27676

> ▶ Learn more about variables in SAP HANA Studio at http://scn.sap.com/docs/DOC-26174

Creating input parameters

Input parameters are used to process a calculation based on the input given by the user at the report execution time. This recipe shows you how to create input parameters.

Getting ready

We create input parameters in an analytic view or a calculation view. Hence to create an input parameter, the analytic/calculation view should be readily available.

How to do it...

In this recipe, we will see how to create input parameters in an analytic view:

1. In the **Semantics** section of the analytic view, select **Create Input Parameter**, as shown in the following screenshot:

2. Now input different parameters such as **Name**, **Parameter Type**, and **Reference Column**, as shown in the following screenshot:

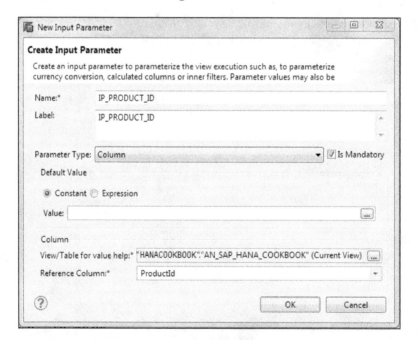

We have selected the input parameter as **Mandatory**. Hence, while the report is executed on top of this view, a value has to be given mandatorily.

How it works...

When an input parameter is created and a report is executed on this model, data will be fetched based on the value we give to the input parameter value.

There are different types of input parameters. The following table explains them:

Type	Description
Column	Use this when the value of a parameter comes from an attribute or a table column
Static List	Use this when the value of a parameter comes from a user-defined list of values
Derived From Table	Use this when the value of a parameter comes from a table column based on some filter conditions and you do not need to provide any input at runtime
Direct	Use this to specify an input parameter as currency and date during the currency conversion

See also

  ▸ Data from SAP HANA with input parameters can be consumed in SAP BW by using Virtual Providers. The related document is available at:

  ❏ http://www.agconsultraining.com/images/download/How%20
     to..%20Consume%20HANA%20Models%20with%20Input%20
     Parameters%20in%20BW%20Virtual%20Providers.pdf

Creating filters

Filters help to reduce the amount of data to be retrieved from a database. This applies both within SAP HANA and also between SAP HANA and the reporting tools.

How to do it...

We will be applying filters as follows:

1. Open the analytic or calculation view, and at the data foundation level, select the field that the filter has to be applied to. Right-click on the field and select **Apply Filter**, as shown in the following screenshot:

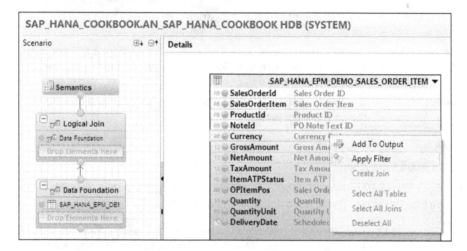

2. Select **Operator** and a filter value to be applied, as shown in the following screenshot:

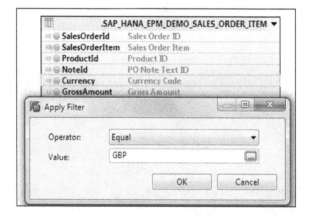

3. After applying the filter, we can see a yellow funnel symbol against the field indicating that the filter has been applied, as shown in the following screenshot:

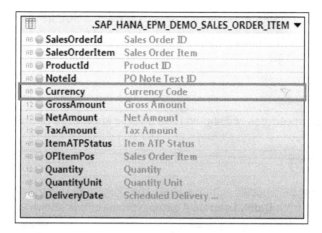

How it works...

The type of filter we created on the field in an analytic/calculation view is called a constraint filter or design-time filter. When such a filter is created on a field, filters will be applied on the data before querying from the database when the view is called. This improves runtime performance. When filters are created on tables and there are joins on those tables, filters will be applied first and then the joins are executed. Data is extracted based on filters; only then are joins executed. This is more helpful when results have to be restricted or filtered based on a single value of a field. For example, we can filter data based on a single year or sales organization.

There's more...

Apart from creating constraint filters, we can also filter default clients while dealing with client-dependent tables. This can be set in two ways:

- ▶ From Navigator Pane, open any information view and change the default client. The change applies to the particular information view alone.

- ▶ From the preferences menu tab of SAP HANA Studio, which makes client default for all the information views created further on.

Creating procedures using SQLScript

Procedures are a set of statements that are reusable. We use SQLScript to create stored procedures. It is required that you know the basics of the SQLScript language before creating procedures.

Getting ready

To create SQLScript procedures, we should have a basic knowledge of SAP HANA SQLScript.

How to do it...

Open SQL Console for the specific schema where the procedure has to be created or create the procedure from **Quick Launch**. A sample procedure is shown in the following code snippet:

```
CREATE PROCEDURE SAP_HANA_COOKBOOK LANGUAGE SQLSCRIPT AS BEGIN
INSERT INTO CUSTOMER_INFO values (1,'CUSTOMER1', 1,'INDIA');
INSERT INTO CUSTOMER_INFO values (2,'CUSTOMER2', 1,'INDIA');
END;
```

How it works...

In the preceding section, we saw a code snippet that will create a procedure. The syntax to create a procedure is shown in the following code:

```
CREATE PROCEDURE <schema>.<procedure_name>
{ ({IN|OUT|INOUT}
param_name data_type {,...})}
{LANGUAGE <LANG>} {SQL SECURITY <MODE>}
{READS SQL DATA {WITH RESULT VIEW <view_name>}} AS
BEGIN
...
END
```

Here:

- ▶ `<schema>` and `<procedure_name>`: `<schema>` is the schema name, and `<procedure_name>` is the name of the procedure. These are mandatory fields.

- ▶ `{IN|OUT|INOUT}`: These are the types of parameters passed into the procedure. These are not mandatory, depends on the parameters that are to be passed to the procedure. `IN` is an input parameter, `OUT` is an output parameter, and `INOUT` acts as both an input and output parameter. If there are any parameters passed, a parameter list has to be included after the type of parameter.

- ▸ {LANGUAGE}: This is the language we use to create the procedure; this is a default field again. By default, SQLScript is the implementation language. As per best practice, it is recommended to define the language while creating the procedure.

- ▸ {SQL SECURITY <MODE>}: This is a type of privilege. By default, this is DEFINER, which means a procedure will be created with the privileges of the user who defines the procedure. There is another mode, INVOKER, which checks the privileges at runtime. This mode depends on the caller of the procedure.

- ▸ {READS SQL DATA}: This is used to make a procedure as a read-only procedure. Defining a procedure as read-only enables it to only call other read-only procedures. The only consideration to made in this case is that neither DDL nor DML statements can be used in the body of the procedure.

- ▸ {WITH RESULT VIEW <view_name>}: The name of the result view can be any valid SQL identifier; it need not be a static name.

See also

- ▸ Learn more about SQLScript procedure templates in SAP HANA at http://www.saphana.com/community/blogs/blog/2013/08/01/sqlscript-procedure-templates-in-sap-hana

Creating decision tables

Decision tables help users who don't have the required SQL knowledge. This recipe tells you how to create decision tables.

Getting ready

Decision tables can be created on a procedure, table, or any SAP HANA model (attribute/analytic/calculation view). Hence, before starting to create decision tables, we must have a SAP HANA artifact.

To create decision tables, the _SYS_REPO user must possess the SELECT, UPDATE, and EXECUTE authorizations with the GRANT option on the schema, which has the table/procedure that is used for the creation of a decision table. If a decision table is created on top of the SAP HANA model, the authorizations discussed should be present on the schema which holds the tables used in the view creation.

How to do it...

Select a package in which a decision table has to be created. Right-click on the package and navigate to **New | Decision Table**, as shown in the following screenshot. We can also create decision tables from the **Quick Launch** menu.

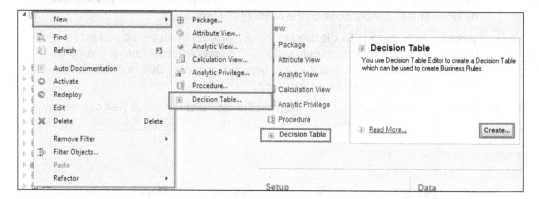

There are two sections in decision tables. They are **Data Foundation** and **Decision Table**. Add the required table into the **Data Foundation** section and select the required fields as attributes, as shown in the following screenshot. In this case, we are taking **ProductId** and **GrossAmount** as attributes. Let us consider that for each product ID, a discount has to be given.

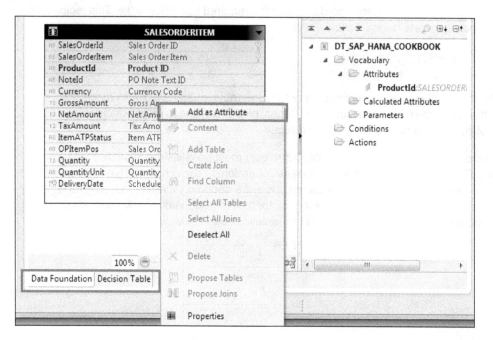

Add fields into **Conditions** and **Actions**, as shown in the following screenshot. The **Conditions** folder holds all the fields that are used for calculation purposes. In this case, **ProductId** will be the condition and **GrossAmount** is the action, as when the condition mentioned for the field in **Conditions** is satisfied, the action maintained in the **Actions** folder will be executed. If we go to the **Decision Table** section without adding fields into **Conditions** or **Actions**, a message will be shown saying that the decision table must have at least one condition and one action. Hence, add the fields into **Conditions** and **Actions** before navigating to the **Decision Table** space.

After the fields are added into **Conditions** and **Actions**, specify the condition values and the appropriate action to be performed under the corresponding fields.

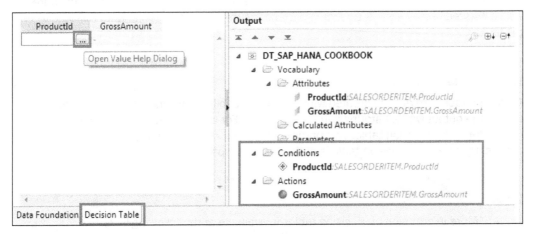

Similarly add all values into **Conditions** and **Actions** based on the requirement and then activate the decision table. For example, in this example we will enter discounts on two products, as shown in the following screenshot:

ProductId	GrossAmount
HT-1000	"GrossAmount" * 0.85
HT-1030	"GrossAmount" * 0.75

On activating the decision table, a database procedure will be created in the `_SYS_BIC` schema, as shown in the following screenshot. This procedure will contain the UPDATE query, which works on the same table used.

```
Parameters  Create Statement
CREATE PROCEDURE "_SYS_BIC"."          /DT_SAP_HANA_COOKBOOK" LANGUAGE SQLSCRIPT AS COUNT139971673315937485625708463363213325 INT :=0 ;
BEGIN
UPDATE "CMANKALA"."SALESORDERITEM" SET "GrossAmount"=
(CASE WHEN "ProductId" = 'HT-1000' THEN "GrossAmount"*0.85
WHEN "ProductId" = 'HT-1030' THEN "GrossAmount"*0.75

ELSE "GrossAmount"
END
);


END;
```

When this procedure is executed, the database table will be updated with the logic we mentioned.

How it works...

Decision tables are mainly intended for business users as most business users will not have knowledge of SQL. Hence, they can create decision tables on their own based on their requirements and test the data. For example, when a user wants to test what happens when he give discounts on objects, he can just create a decision table with the information and check the report. As discussed earlier, when a decision table is activated, a new procedure will be created in the _SYS_BIC schema. Executing this procedure will update the data in the table.

There's more...

A decision table can also be created with a return capability. This enables us to just return data in the output without storing it in the database. For this, we have to create a new parameter in the decision table. This parameter is used while assigning values to the actions. By default, a decision table is of the UPDATE type.

See also

▸ More information on decision tables is available at the following links:

  ❑ http://scn.sap.com/community/developer-center/hana/
    blog/2013/01/11/what-can-you-do-with-decision-tables-
    in-sap-hana-sp05

  ❑ http://scn.sap.com/community/developer-center/hana/
    blog/2013/10/09/decision-table-in-sap-hana--concept

  ❑ http://scn.sap.com/community/developer-center/hana/
    blog/2013/10/09/decision-table-on-hana-database-tables

6
User Management

In this chapter, we will cover:

- ▶ Creating users
- ▶ Creating roles
- ▶ Assigning roles to users
- ▶ Restricting access to data – creating analytic privileges
- ▶ Securing logging in to SAP HANA – authentication methods
- ▶ Securing logging in to SAP HANA – privileges

Introduction

This chapter deals with the basics of the administration part, but covers important topics in the view of certification. We will cover how to create users and roles, assign the created roles to the users, and the creation of analytic privileges. This chapter also covers the types of privileges and authentication methods available in SAP HANA.

Creating users

User IDs are required to log in to a SAP HANA database. This recipe is all about creating users. Let us see how to create users in SAP HANA Studio.

Getting ready

Only database users with the USER ADMIN system privilege are allowed to create another database user. The name of the user should not be the same as the existing user/role/ schema. For example, a few users such as SYS, _SYS_BIC, SYSTEM, and _SYS_REPO are delivered with SAP HANA.

How to do it...

We can create user IDs in two ways: using the GUI method in SAP HANA Studio or using the SQL code. This recipe is about creating users by the GUI method.

Let's follow the given steps:

1. Expand the Security folder in the system where a user has to be created.

2. Expand the **Users** menu, right-click on **Users**, and click on **New User**, as shown in the following screenshot.

3. Upon doing this, a new screen appears. In this screen, give the name of the user to be created. Authentication can be provided by passwords, the Kerberos mechanism, or the **Security Assertion Markup Language** (**SAML**) mechanism. Here, we will go with passwords. Give a password and assign roles and privileges accordingly.

4. Click on **Execute**. This will produce a pop-up message that states **User successfully created**.

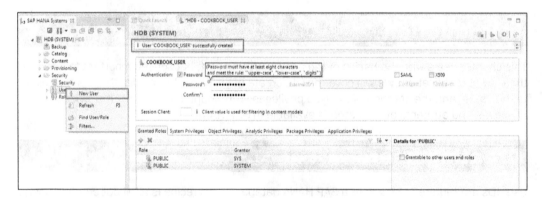

How it works...

A database user is mandatory to log in to the SAP HANA system, because when we add a new system in SAP HANA Studio, it asks for user credentials. Object visibility (schemas) and actions (SELECT/INSERT/UPDATE/DELETE) depends on the roles/privileges the user has. We must consider the following points before creating a user:

- We should know the purpose of the user we are creating; only then can we assign roles/privileges.
- When a user is created, a schema will be created with the same name. The user created will have all privileges on that schema.
- Only database users with system privileges, such as USER ADMIN, are allowed to create another database user. The name of the user should not be the same as the existing user/role/schema.
- By default, a few users such as SYS, _SYS_BIC, SYSTEM, and _SYS_REPO are delivered with SAP HANA. The name of the user we create should not conflict with these, and the privileges on these schemas have to be given carefully as these schemas are system schemas that contain the metadata of all schemas.
- SYSTEM is the power user who will have privileges for all the schemas. This user is delivered with SAP HANA.
- The PUBLIC role has to be given to all the new users. This is the minimum role required to access the SAP HANA database.

There's more...

We can also create users using SQL Console. The syntax for the code to create users is as follows:

```
CREATE USER <user_name> [PASSWORD <password>]
[IDENTIFIED EXTERNALLY AS <external_identity>]
[WITH IDENTITY <provider_identity>] [<set_user_parameters>]
```

After users are created, we can grant roles/privileges accordingly. We can modify users and change privileges later if need be.

See also

- A video that explains the creation of users in SAP HANA is available at http://www.saphana.com/docs/DOC-2279

Creating roles

A role is a set of privileges. When the same set of privileges have to be assigned to all users, we create a role with all the required privileges and then assign this role to the users. We can assign a role to users or other roles. This recipe covers the creation of roles.

Getting ready

We must possess the ROLE ADMIN system privilege to grant roles to other roles and users.

How to do it...

Roles can be created in two ways: the GUI method or the SQL code, just as we did for user creation in the previous recipe. This section covers how to create roles using the GUI method.

Let's follow the given steps:

1. Expand the `Security` folder in the system where a role has to be created.

2. Expand the **Roles** menu, right-click on **Roles**, and click on **New Role**, as shown in the following screenshot:

3. In the next screen, give the name of the role to be created. Assign the required roles/privileges that this role should hold.

4. Click on **Execute**. This will produce a pop-up message that states **Role successfully created**.

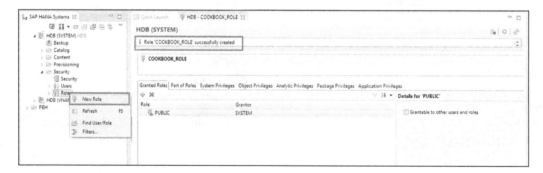

How it works...

A role is a set of privileges that can be granted to the other role or user. Upon assigning a role to the user, they will be restricted to objects/data based on the privileges that the role holds. The default roles that come with the installation of SAP HANA are **PUBLIC**, **MODELING**, **CONTENT_ADMIN**, **MONITORING**, and **SUPPORT**.

There's more...

A role can be created using SQL code. The code syntax for role creation is as follows:

```
CREATE ROLE <role_name>
```

See also

▸ A video that explains the creation of roles in SAP HANA is available at http://www.saphana.com/docs/DOC-2280

Assigning roles to users

Roles created can be assigned to users, thus providing authorization to users for objects/data. In this recipe, we will see how to assign roles to users.

Getting ready

In order to assign roles to users, we should have roles and users created readily.

How to do it...

We will be assigning roles to users as follows:

1. Open the user from the `Security` folder.
2. From the **Granted Roles** tab, add a role by searching for the created role. In our example, the role is **COOKBOOK_ROLE**, as shown in the following screenshot.

3. Then activate the user by clicking on **Deploy**.

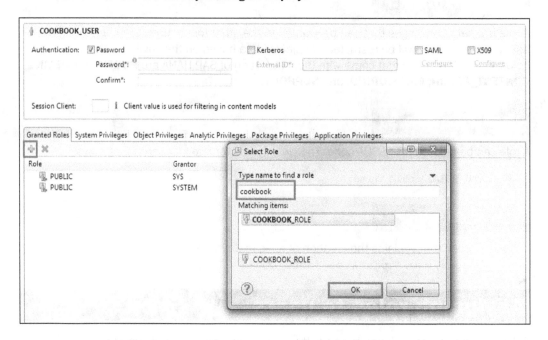

How it works...

When a role is assigned to a user, the privileges and other roles that the newly created role holds are inherited by the user that we assign the role to. Thus, when we use that user ID and start modeling in SAP HANA Studio, all the privileges come to action and thereby the user gets all the assigned authorizations that are inherited as a part of the assigned role.

There's more...

The same set of actions as assigning roles to users can be done with the GRANT SQL statement.

See also

▶ Check the syntax of the GRANT statement with complete information on privileges at `http://help.sap.com/hana/html/sql_grant.html`

Restricting access to data – creating analytic privileges

Analytic privileges are used to restrict data access to users. We create analytic privileges on top of the SAP HANA model. We select the attributes and also the set of values that these privileges have to be applied to. Finally, we assign analytic privileges to users. This recipe explains how to create analytic privileges.

Getting ready

Analytic privileges are created on top of the SAP HANA model, that is, the attribute/analytic/calculation view. Hence, to start creating analytic privileges, we should have SAP HANA models ready in hand.

How to do it...

To start creating analytic privileges, follow the given steps:

1. From the Navigator Pane, right-click on the package (in which the analytic privilege has to be created) from the **Content** folder and go to **New | Analytic Privilege**, as shown in the following screenshot:

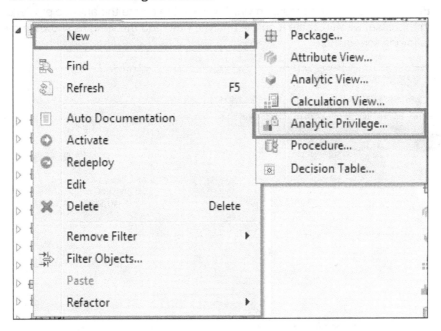

2. Give a name and description and click on **Next**, as shown in the following screenshot:

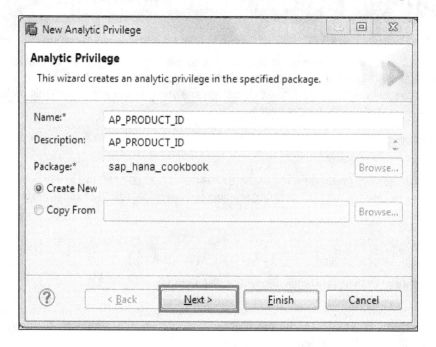

3. Browse and select the model on which we want to create the analytic privilege. In this case, we will create it on the analytic view. Add the view, as shown in the following screenshot:

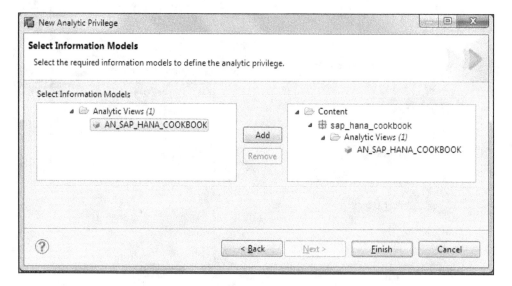

4. In the next screen, select **Add** under **Associated Attributes Restrictions**. Select a field for which the data access has to be restricted. Here, we select **ProductId**, as shown in the following screenshot:

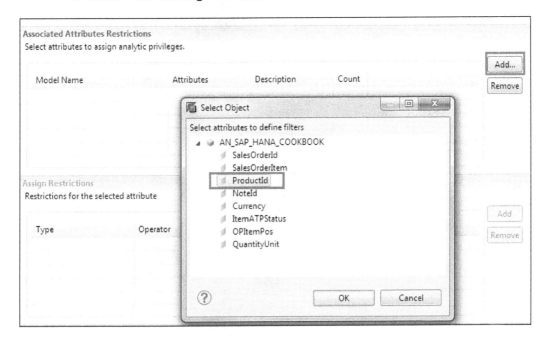

5. Now, from the **Assign Restrictions** section, click on **Add**. Select **Type** and **Operator**. To assign a value, click on the help dialog so that all the values in that column will be displayed, as shown in the following screenshot. Select a value and click on **OK**.

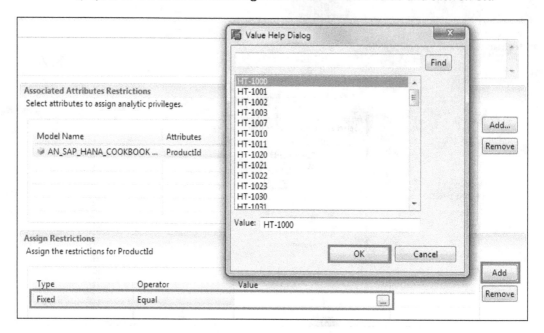

6. Now activate the analytic privilege. With this step, we have created the analytic privilege.

7. We should assign this to the user. From the `Security` folder, select a user that this analytic privilege has to be assigned to. In this case, we assign it to **COOKBOOK_USER**. Go to the **Analytic Privileges** tab and click on **Add**. For this example, search for the analytic privilege, **AP_PRODUCT_ID** and click on **OK**, as shown in the following screenshot. Activate the user.

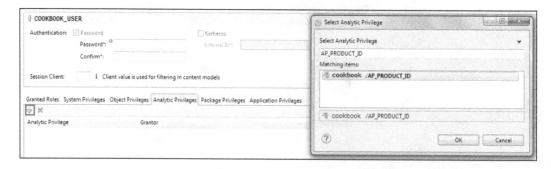

How it works...

When a user executes a report and the control comes to SAP HANA, it checks for the authorizations and privileges that the user has. In the case of analytic privileges, after we assign it to a user, they will be restricted to view only the data of those particular values. Analytical privileges helps to restrict row-level access to the data.

For example, in the following screenshot, the user will have access to the entire set of data before the analytic privilege is assigned. We can see that there are 71 distinct values for **ProductId**.

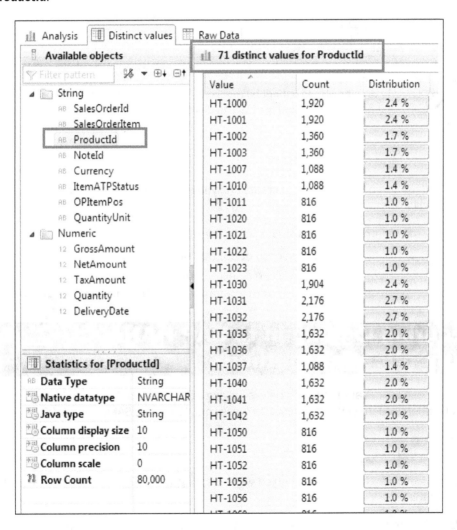

After the analytic privilege is assigned, the data for only **ProductId HT-100** is available to the user, as shown in the following screenshot:

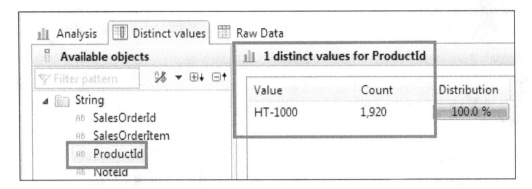

 Analytic privileges cannot be modified. We can activate them only once. If it has to be modified, we have to delete it and create it again.

See also

▸ Videos demonstrating how to create analytic privileges and other examples are available at:

  ❑ http://www.saphana.com/docs/DOC-2292

  ❑ http://scn.sap.com/docs/DOC-41261

  ❑ http://scn.sap.com/community/hana-in-memory/
    blog/2012/05/30/user-management-analytic-privileges

Securing logging in to SAP HANA – authentication methods

Each database user is authenticated before logging in to a system. For this process, we have several authentication methods: username/password, Kerberos, SAML, and X509.

How to do it...

An authentication method can be enabled while creating/modifying the user. Let us see how to achieve this:

1. If we are creating a new user and we want to apply an authentication method in the same screen where we give the password, there are authentication methods available. Select one of them.

2. If authentication has to be applied for an existing user, open the `Security` folder from the Navigator Pane, expand the **Users** menu, and open the user that has to be modified. Select an authentication method and click on the green arrow button on the top right-hand side of the screen (**Deploy**).

The following screenshot shows the screen where we can select the authentication method:

How it works...

The most commonly used authentication method is username/password. For each user, a password is created. Thus, before logging in to a SAP HANA database, the user must provide the password.

The Kerberos authentication provider can be used to authenticate SAP HANA users to access data directly from SQLDBC and JDBC database clients in the same network. We can also access SAP HANA from frontend applications such as SAP BO using Kerberos delegation. The drawback with Kerberos authentication is that the HTTP access is not supported by SAP HANA XS.

SAML stands for Security Assertion Markup Language. We can use SAML for authentication purposes. Users can access SAP HANA using the SAML bearer assertion from the ODBC/JDBC database clients. For users accessing through HTTP, SAP HANA acts as a service provider.

Users can be authenticated by client certificates signed by the Certification Authority (CA) to provide HTTP access to SAP HANA by means of SAP HANA XS. These certificates are stored in the SAP HANA XS trust store. To implement X509 client certificates, we must configure support for SSL in advance, and the user mentioned in the certificate must exist in the database too.

See also

▶ *SAP HANA One Security Guide*, which explains security concepts is available at http://help.sap.com/hana_one/SAP_HANA_One_Security_Guide_en.pdf

Securing logging in to SAP HANA – privileges

We need certain authorizations to work on SAP HANA models. In order to get the required authorizations, there are privileges. This recipe covers the available privileges.

Getting ready

When we access the SAP HANA database, privileges to data have to be maintained. Privileges can be maintained at different levels.

How to do it...

There are four types of privileges in order to authorize the data in the system: SQL privilege, system privilege, package privilege, and analytic privilege.

Follow the given steps to authorize the data in the system:

1. Open the user that the privileges on objects are to be given to.
2. Go to the corresponding user in the user maintenance screen and add the required privilege.
3. As an example, we will assign all privileges on the **SAP_HANA_EPM_DEMO** schema to our **COOKBOOK_USER**, as shown in the following screenshot:

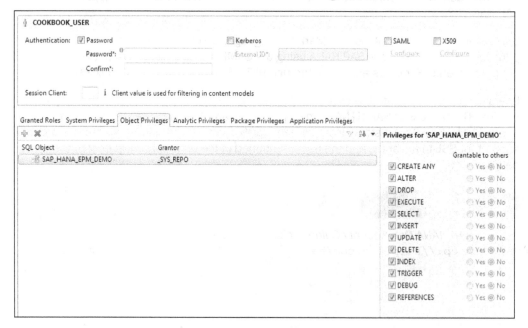

Similarly, we can assign different privileges to the user, thereby providing access to the data.

How it works...

SQL privileges are used to restrict access to the database objects and the dependent objects. We can assign SQL privileges on any object to users and roles.

System privileges are used for administrative tasks; these privileges can be assigned to users and roles.

Package privileges are used to restrict access to repository objects such as packages. Packages contain information views (attribute/analytic/calculation) and analytic privileges. In order to have access to the package and work on it, respective package privileges have to be assigned to the users.

Analytic privileges are used to implement row-level security to the data. These are applied at the processing time of the user query. We have to create analytic privileges in advance to assign them to users or roles.

Introduction to SAP HANA

In this appendix, we will cover:

- ▸ Explaining traditional databases and bottlenecks
- ▸ Introducing technology and hardware innovations
- ▸ Looking into versions and technical requirements
- ▸ Describing why to go with SAP HANA
- ▸ Looking into SAP HANA features
- ▸ Comparing BWA and SAP HANA

Introduction

This appendix explains the features of SAP HANA, compares them with other traditional databases, and explains the bottlenecks currently faced by users. We will go through the groundbreaking technology innovations that have led to the innovation of the SAP HANA database and see how the database supports analyzing real-time data even in huge chunks. We will also see why the SAP HANA database is a good choice when other databases with similar features are available.

HANA stands for **High-Performance Analytic Appliance**. SAP HANA is a combination of hardware and software, and is therefore an appliance. SAP HANA supports column- and row-level storage. We can store and perform analytics on a huge amount of real-time, non-aggregated transactional data. Hence, HANA acts as both a database and a warehousing tool, which helps in making decisions at the right time.

Explaining traditional databases and bottlenecks

Traditional databases are arranged by fields, records, and files. A field is defined as a single piece of information; a record is one complete set of fields; and a file is a collection of records. This recipe explains traditional databases and the bottlenecks in using them.

How it works...

Let us look at the features of traditional databases in this section.

Traditional databases

The traditional databases available today support only the storage of data. The data may be coming in from a variety of data sources, that is, data may be in an unstructured format or from data marts, operational datastores, data warehouses, and so on. Every year, a massive amount of data is being created, and for an organization, it is always critical to make decisions based on this big chunk of data. There are a few challenges, such as cost, latency, architecture, and complexity, in accessing these databases for analyzing Big Bata in real time. These result in inadequate access to complete data, and there will be a lag in gathering data and analyzing it.

Let us consider the following simple example to get an idea of the amount of data created on the Internet every minute:

Source: http://mashable.com/2012/06/22/data-created-every-minute/

With the evolution of e-commerce, it is very necessary for organizations to remain competitive. To achieve this, the data of the clients who visit a company's website has to be captured and analyzed. This analysis helps the company draw two major findings:

▸ Customer behavior can be analyzed by analyzing customers' usage patterns. This helps companies understand the types of customers visiting their websites.

▸ Customer satisfaction can be increased by catering to their requirements. These can be easily found out by analyzing the usage pattern of their company website.

When the preceding points are considered, it is a huge business advantage, and effective ways of advertising can be determined. We can achieve this huge advantage using **clickstreams**; organizations have already understood the importance of clickstreams and are in the process of building Business Intelligence based on this clickstream data, which helps monitor the data, analyze it, and make decisions. There are several techniques to achieve better results in data recording and analyzing. One of the techniques is usage of data mining, column-oriented DBMS, and integrated OLAP systems, in combination with clickstreams.

It is a very well-known fact that data never sleeps; creation of data is continuous and will increase with population growth. Analyzing data in huge amounts in real time is only a dream when working with traditional databases.

There's more...

Having looked at the features of traditional databases, now let us see the bottlenecks in using them.

Bottlenecks

As mentioned in the beginning of the section, there are a few challenges in traditional databases, such as latency, the cost involved, and complexity in accessing databases.

Latency

Databases store data in secondary storage devices. When applications are built on databases to analyze the data, disk I/O operation is the main problem in data throughput. The CPU waits for the data to be loaded from the disk to a CPU cache, which leads to very high latency. There were many changes made to existing systems to minimize disk access, which in turn have minimized the number of pages loaded to the main memory when processing a query. The following diagram shows the evolution of memory bandwidth and CPU clock speed over the years:

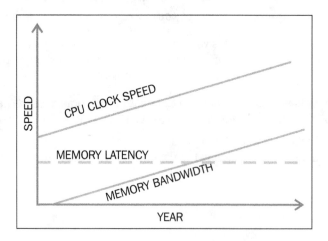

With the advent of multicore CPUs and the declining cost of memory, computer architecture has changed in the recent past by hosting an entire database in the RAM.

In the current scenario, multicore CPUs (multiple CPUs on one chip or in one package) have become standard, which enables fast communication between processor cores. With the advent of these changes in the technology, main memory is not a limited resource now. There are servers that can have a system memory of up to 2 TB. This helps us to store an entire database in the RAM itself. The processors used in these servers have up to 64 cores and, in the near future, they are expected to get 128 cores. When the number of cores increases, CPUs can process huge amounts of data simultaneously. When this happens, a performance bottleneck is considered to have occurred between the CPU cache and main memory, and not for disk I/O operations.

Cost

In mainframes, transactional data and applications are stored on the same system. This is due to the fact that applications, operating systems, and the underlying databases share the same hardware resources. This means that we can't process transactions and reports concurrently. The problem here is cost. If we want to scale, we need another mainframe, which includes high cost. The cost of memory has come down drastically. This has brought on a revolution in increasing the size of memory. The following graph shows the fall of memory price over the years:

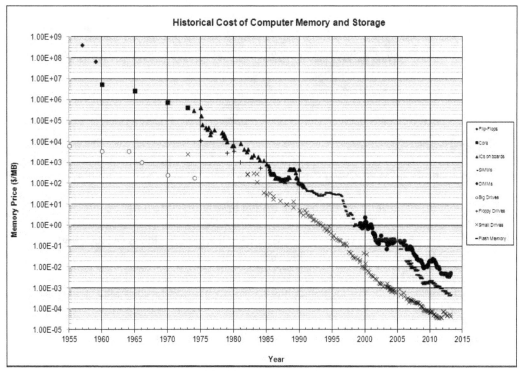

Source: http://www.jcmit.com/mem2013.htm

From the preceding graph, it is very clear that the cost of memory has come down tremendously and is predicted to go down further in the near future.

Architecture

Present day applications running on traditional databases follow a 3-tier architecture. This is because databases are not capable of doing any calculations that involve complex logic or huge amounts of data; they are only capable of storing the data. There is a need for one more layer between the database and presentation layers—the application layer—to take care of all the calculations, based on which business logics from the base fields are implemented, as shown in the following diagram:

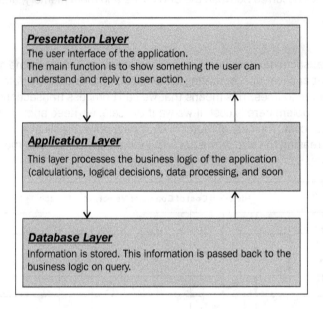

Let us look at each layer in detail:

- ▶ **Presentation Layer**: This is the top-most layer and allows users to manipulate data so that they can input it for querying. This data input from users is passed on to the database layer through the application layer and the results are passed back to the application layer to implement business logics. The presentation layer can be anything—the web browser, SAP GUI, SAP BEx, SAP Business Objects, and so on. These tools will be installed on individual client machines.

- ▶ **Application Layer**: This layer is also called the business layer. All the business logic will be executed in this layer. It controls the application's functionality by performing detailed processing. This can be installed on one machine or distributed across more than one system.

> ▶ **Database Layer**: This layer receives data from the business layer and performs the required operation from the database. It contains database servers that store the data. Data is stored independently of application layers or business logics. The database layer remains as an internal interface and is not exposed to the end users. The application layer has to access the data in the database only through this layer.

See also

> ▶ The basics of RDBMS concepts is available at `http://www.srnr.arizona.edu/rnr/rnr417/rdbms.pdf`

Introducing technology and hardware innovations

Today's technology requires trade-off. In the present-day scenario, five factors are considered in analyzing data—the depth of data, its broadness, whether or not it is in real time, the simplicity of the data, and the retrieval speed of data. This section explains these factors and the innovations that came on the hardware side.

How it works...

Let us walk through different concepts that are very important in analyzing data.

Depth of data

Depth of data includes the granularity of data. This factor mainly depends on how deep we are diving into analyzing the data. For example, when a global head queries the data, it will hit on the entire set of data. Let us say a regional manager of a particular country is querying the data; in this case, only a set of data will be hit. The analysis made is the same, but the amount of data being queried differs. Once the query is obtained, there will be situations where data has to be sliced and diced. Let us consider that the query run by the global/regional head is on a single year's data. Now, we can also start drilling down the report up to a single day. This involves huge amounts of data. The queries run may be simple or more interactive with the user.

Broadness

The data we are dealing with need not necessarily be of the same data types. So, in a very simple way, we can categorize this as big data. The data may comprise text, pictures, video, and so on. When a query hits on such a huge amount and variety of data, it becomes difficult to combine the bits set to give only a small set of data.

Real time

The analysis should be running in real time rather than post-mortem. Decisions taken based on real-time data will be more productive compared to the post-mortem analysis. To achieve this, data has to be continuously replicated into SAP HANA in real time so that queries are run over it.

Simplicity

The data has to be prepared before presenting it to the user. There will be scenarios where we may need to build pre-aggregates and also tune the data. The simpler the data is, the faster it can be accessed. When we go on increasing the complexity, it takes more time to retrieve the results.

Retrieval speed

The data should be retrieved very quickly. When we are interacting with the data, results should be displayed on-the-fly without any latency. When we aim at a very low retrieval time for the data, all the preceding factors should be at a minimum.

With present-day technologies available, we can have optimal results in terms of a single factor only; that is, we can only go in-depth on large varieties of data. In doing this, we cannot expect results to be fast, and the same results cannot be run on real-time data or a complex set of data. To get the results very quickly, the data set has to be very simple.

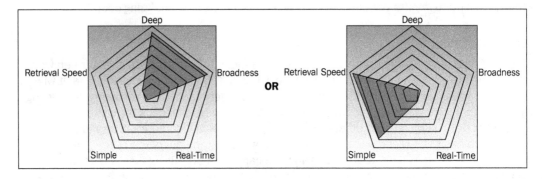

To overcome all these problems and obtain the best results, we need an innovative, groundbreaking technology.

There's more...

There has been dramatic improvement in hardware economics and technological innovations. This has made it possible for SAP to deliver SAP HANA. Hence, SAP HANA enables real-time analysis of data, with very high performance levels as all the data resides completely within in-memory business applications. SAP HANA is a hybrid in-memory database that supports data storage with two different techniques—row or column.

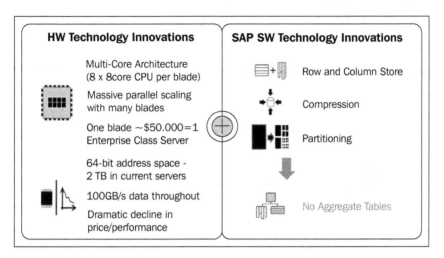

Multicore CPUs

In the initial development stages of technology, the core area in processors started decreasing, increasing the cache. This was the trend during the period between Pentium-I and Pentium-IV, but not after that. Instead, the number of cores in a single processor was increased and multicore processors evolved. We can compare a core of a processor to the brain of a human being. We use our brain to do all the activities in our day-to-day lives. The same brain takes care of all the activities. When we are doing one activity, we cannot do another with the same level of concentration. Similarly, when a processor is busy performing one operation, it cannot take up another. Imagine how it would be if we were to have multiple brains. We could allocate each brain for separate activities. This is exactly what happens in a multicore processor.

Each core can take up a separate operation, thereby increasing the capabilities of a computer. This is a revolutionary change in the field of processors. Moore's law states that the number of transistors on integrated circuits doubles approximately every two years. Based on this law, it has been predicted that if the current trend continues to 2020, the number of transistors will reach 32 billion.

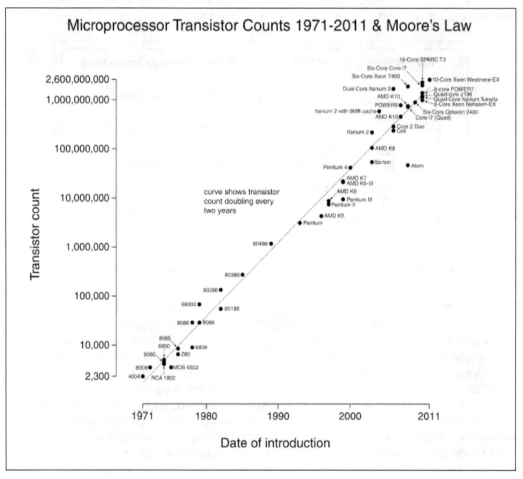

Source: http://en.wikipedia.org/wiki/File:Transistor_Count_and_
Moore%27s_Law_-_2011.svg

Since the beginning of the year 2000, there has been a drastic change in the processing power and speed of processors. Modern systems that are in use today have an architecture that can support up to eight separate CPUs, each being able to contain 12 separate cores. This change in processing power should be used to get the best throughput for both analytical and transactional applications. It is very important for enterprise applications that their work be reduced and they be developed in such a way that parallelization is always achieved. Parallelization has to be achieved at different levels, including the application being run on an application server until the query execution in the database system. Multithreading helps process multiple queries at a time so that the applications don't halt when there are more queries to be processed. Each CPU core will take care of a single process. Hence, when we have more core CPUs, the system response time is optimal as multicore CPUs process any number of queries effectively.

Parallel processing

Multicore CPUs also help achieve higher CPU execution speeds. With multicore CPUs, calling parallel algorithms in databases is possible; therefore, all the available computing resources can be utilized. As SAP HANA supports column-based storage, it is easy to execute operations in parallel using multiple processor cores. This is possible as data will be partitioned column-wise. Hence, queries can be run in parallel on different columns. When queries hit multiple columns, different processor cores work on different columns so that final results are aggregated. In the case where a query hits only a single column, it is split into several sections, each of which will be handled by a different processor core.

Data compression

We store all data in the main memory. Hence, it is of high priority that data be compressed and stored for the efficient utilization of memory; if not, it leads to very high costs. With columnar storage, high compression rates are possible; typically, a compression rate of 10 times the original can be achieved compared to that in row storage systems, because when we sort the values in a column, several contiguous values will be placed adjacent to each other. In this scenario, compression techniques such as cluster coding, run-length encoding, and dictionary coding are used.

See also

▸ A paper on cache-conscious data-structures is available at `http://research.microsoft.com/en-us/um/people/trishulc/papers/ccds.pdf`

Looking into versions and technical requirements

In this section, we will be looking into the two main flavors in SAP HANA—Enterprise HANA and SAP NetWeaver BW powered by SAP HANA. We will also discuss the technical differences and requirements for both the versions.

How it works...

In this section, let us understand how enterprise HANA and SAP NetWeaver BW powered by HANA operate.

Enterprise HANA

Enterprise HANA is also known as Standalone HANA. We know that HANA is fundamentally a database which can enable a number of solutions. In this version of the product, though, SAP HANA acts more like an appliance solution; we have to look at the entire set of components all at once. We need to look at the hardware, the SAP HANA database, the specific software components that we'll be required to implement, the modeling studio, the BI tools, and the administration of SAP HANA.

Although the standalone SAP HANA version is called an "appliance" solution, keep in mind that this is not one fully contained plug and play solution. SAP HANA is not plug and play in any scenario and certainly not in the standalone version. When we purchase Standalone SAP HANA, we get the following tools:

- SAP In-Memory Computing Studio
- SAP Host Agent 7.2
- SAP CAR 7.10
- Sybase Replication Server 15
- SAP HANA Load Controller 1.00
- SAP Landscape Transformation

We can't just implement this set of technology because we still need hardware, a BI tool or the intention to access data via Microsoft Excel, and a data integration tool. There is no requirement that the source systems (the systems where the data comes from) for our SAP HANA databases be SAP environments, but the implications of our choice of source system will determine which data loading tool we can work with and our options for those tools. Next, we'll discuss both the technical and skill requirements for a company implementing the standalone version of SAP HANA. We'll conclude the section with a high-level overview of what a project plan should involve.

Technical requirements

The components we require for the standalone version of SAP HANA will be the same as those that SAP HANA for BW would require; but with this version, we have to build everything from scratch. The architecture in this case looks like that shown in the following diagram:

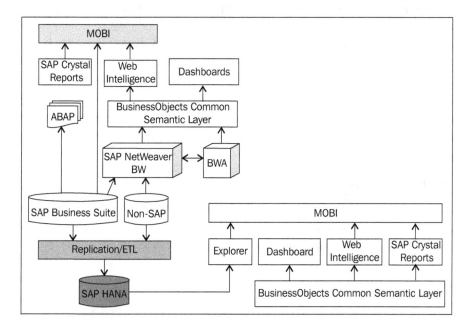

The architecture in the preceding diagram basically enables us to create new reporting and analytical solutions for our transaction data. However, it also allows us to take an additional data set from those transaction systems that are timelier, more detailed, and have more volume, and bring them into the SAP HANA database.

MOBI is the mobile version of the SAP BO reporting tools. A few reporting tools such as WebI and Crystal Reports can be accessed from mobile devices as well.

SAP NetWeaver BW powered by SAP HANA

BW on HANA is the first significant step toward achieving SAP's goal of being a major player in the database space and having its transaction systems running on a SAP HANA database in short order. Running SAP HANA for SAP NetWeaver BW allows us to leverage what SAP has dubbed as the **Massive Parallel Processing** (**MPP**) capabilities of SAP HANA to query and report against the massive BW cubes and get results in subseconds. SAP HANA is much faster than the regular relational databases such as Oracle or Microsoft SQL Server. This helps in better performance of the data warehouse, and therefore the reports will run much faster. This version of SAP HANA is really the starting point from where SAP is progressing toward its long-term goals of using SAP HANA as the underlying database for existing solutions. By including SAP HANA in our SAP NetWeaver BW environment, we are actually removing the Oracle or DB2 database that we've been using all these years. In this scenario, we don't have to design everything from scratch as we do with the standalone version of SAP HANA. Instead, we simply replace our existing database with SAP HANA.

Technical requirements

The following diagram shows the architecture for SAP NetWeaver BW powered by SAP HANA:

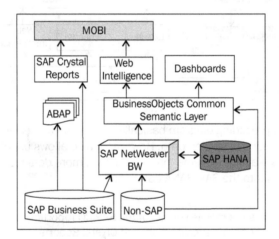

We don't see much difference between SAP HANA for SAP NetWeaver BW and Enterprise HANA. In this scenario, we see that SAP HANA is now directly attached to SAP NetWeaver BW. This tells us that SAP HANA is a database, not a separate instance. It is not required to build new ETL layers or design a data model from scratch. We can use our existing BW models and structures. Those are all good things, but there's one big catch—there are version requirements for this level of SAP HANA. Because we are using SAP HANA as a database for our SAP NetWeaver BW system, this BW system must be of a certain version and level. The SAP BusinessObjects BI system must also be of a certain version and level. At the time of writing this book, we must be on SAP NetWeaver BW 7.3 (Unicode) with SAP BusinessObjects 4.0 (if we are using the SAP BusinessObjects toolset). The first thing we need to determine when assessing how quickly, easily, and at what cost we can implement SAP HANA for BW, is whether we need a system upgrade first. The next thing we need to look at is our hardware for our existing SAP NetWeaver BW system. It must be compatible with our new SAP HANA database. As with the standalone version of SAP HANA, we'll need hardware that can handle the needs and power of the SAP HANA database.

There's more...

There are more things to know, which are discussed in this section.

Server

SAP HANA runs on the **SUSE Linux Enterprise Server** (**SLES**). These are big rack-mount systems that take up to eight CPUs and 80 cores to work. We can also basically stack these on top of each other for our scale-out options. We can purchase this software on the Internet from the big vendors, but we may also be able to negotiate a deal with our regular hardware partner. There are showcase systems that are of 100 TB.

RAM

A lot of RAM is required and should be matched to the CPUs. 20 cores allow 256 GB RAM, resulting in a maximum of 1 TB of RAM for current CPUs.

Log storage

The trick to the quick recovery of a SAP HANA system that goes down—for example, due to power loss—is the ability to quickly restore the data via the logs.

Data storage

The requirement for data storage is four times that of RAM. On all of the certified single-node configurations, there is cheap SAS direct storage. We need this so we can power down the appliance and perform actions such as backups. For multinode configurations, some form of shared storage is required—either SAN or a local storage replicated using IBM's GPFS (General Parallel File System) type of solution.

So, when we're looking at the hardware side of implementation costs and planning, we need to determine whether or not our existing hardware will meet the preceding requirements. We'll also have to make sure our hardware is compatible with the server versions that SAP HANA requires, which means we might have to look at a new series of hardware. If that is the case, the good news is that we'll need much less hardware than our current solution requires because of the compression ratios. Our hardware vendor can help us decide how much of our existing hardware can be leveraged for this new solution. We'll also need to plan for racking and stacking the box, just like with the standalone version of SAP HANA. On average, this will take a couple of days when we factor in the knowledge transfer to our existing support team.

After we have established SAP HANA as our database, we'll likely want to change a few things about our SAP NetWeaver BW system. We should first get rid of all of the aggregates on our cubes. Why would we do this when aggregates have been a necessary evil all along? Aggregates on a traditional, non-SAP HANA BW system are about precalculating certain results so that we do not have to spend time on it during query and report processing to compile and calculate those results. Aggregates deal with bad performance, or at least slow performance, particularly when our BW cubes and data sets start to get very large. After we convert our SAP NetWeaver BW to a SAP HANA database, we'll no longer need those aggregates to precalculate and make accommodations for system performance. As far as SAP HANA is concerned, aggregates are completely unnecessary overhead and add no value whatsoever. Getting rid of aggregates will also improve our data loading because we won't have to roll everything up to aggregates anymore!

Finally, we may wonder what we need to do with our BW cubes after we implement SAP HANA. We don't have to do much, but we do need to convert our BW cubes to SAP HANA cubes. This simple process allows the cubes to be stretched across the SAP HANA database in the new columnar format, which also reduces some of the overall size of the cubes themselves.

See also

- SAP HANA Versions – Service Packs
- SAP HANA Editions

Describing why you should use SAP HANA

This section explains why should we use SAP HANA even though there are many databases on the market.

Getting ready

SAP HANA is a real-time applications platform that provides a multipurpose, in-memory appliance. Decision makers in the organization can gain instant insight into business operations. As all the data available can be analyzed, they can react to the business conditions rapidly to make decisions. The following are the advantages of SAP HANA:

- **Real Time**: One can access the most granular information from both SAP and non-SAP sources within moments of it changing.

- **Applications**: SAP HANA is the future for the entire SAP portfolio of products and solutions, unlocking new insights, predicting issues before they occur, and allowing you to plan for scenarios at the speed of thought.

- **Platform**: SAP HANA is fundamentally different from anything else on the market. The SAP HANA platform will power current products, such as Business Warehouse, and new trends, such as mobility, for which fast analysis and advanced computation is required.

How it works...

Now it's time to look at the differences between traditional and SAP HANA databases.

Traditional versus in-memory

The following table distinguishes between the approaches of traditional and SAP HANA databases toward different scenarios:

Key features for comparison	Traditional approach	Next generation approach
Volume of data	Row store, compression (disk-based). Data duplication through aggregates, caching, and compression.	Column store and compression (in-memory-based) addressed by keeping all data in-memory. No data duplication using non-materialized views (no aggregates).
Information latency	ETL leads to batch loading and the delayed availability of information. Additional delay in latency by rolling up aggregates and caching.	Addressed by replication server. Non-materialized views (no aggregates required). Quick performance on all the data (not relying on in-memory caches).

Key features for comparison	Traditional approach	Next generation approach
Computation speeds	Addressed by row store and caching the data to memory.	Addressed by column storage and the full in-memory dataset. The calculation happens in-memory, that is, in the database tier instead of the application tier.
Flexibility and robustness	Disk-based solutions provide limited flexibility (changing data models or re-aligning hierarchies requires changes to aggregates, caches, and so on).	HANA allows us to change our data model anytime as changes occur in-memory and is not limited by disk persistence first.
Data governance	Duplicate versions of data in a layered, scalable architecture involve costly reconciliation activities.	Provides a single version of the truth.
Application platform	Only for analytical use cases (not transactional).	Targets applications that combine both OLAP and OLTP.

There's more...

Let us also see how data marts exist in Business Intelligence today. We initially store the data in a staging area. Then, we store the same data redundantly in different layers. Data in each layer differs by the way it is stored such as operational datastores, after applying business logics, and aggregated data. In this case, data has to hop through multiple layers. So, it takes a lot of time to reach end users for decision-making. The data is useless when it is not available in time for decision-making.

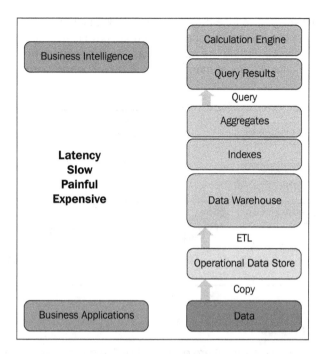

Let's go through a detailed analysis of this scenario. Several layers exist between operational datastores and the application layers, in which reports are executed by the users. Based on these reports, decisions are made to run the business. All the middle-level layers, such as warehouses, data marts, cubes, and universes, are involved only in data copying and management processes. Data has to hop through all these layers to reach reports.

There are exponential changes in terms of memory, but not in terms of disk access. Disc access speed is almost the same as it was in the past as there are aerodynamic limits—disks would fly off the spindle at very high speeds.

Hence, data storage in the main memory helped reduce the cost of disk access. But the cost involved in storage memory is too high. With time, the cost of memory came down, making memory cheaper than in the past. So, databases are designed in such a way that all the data resides in the main memory.

Why choose SAP HANA only to reduce the costs involved with all the layers? As an in-memory database that supports the real-time processing of data, data is aggregated and processed in the memory itself, thereby getting the results at an amazing speed. Results can be shown on-the-fly so that middle-level management related to IT can be replaced for fulfilling the new requests from users.

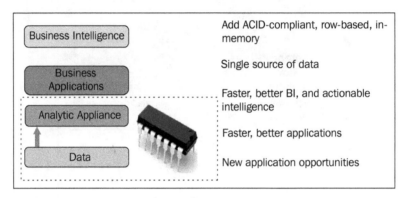

See also

▶ The ACID properties in DBMS are explained well in this presentation available at `http://www.google.co.in/url?sa=t&rct=j&q=&esrc=s&frm=1&source=web&cd=1&ved=0CCgQFjAA&url=http%3A%2F%2Fieor.berkeley.edu%2F~goldberg%2Fcourses%2FF04%2F215%2F215-Database-Recovery.ppt&ei=5_6oUqPUJMv9rAfumoCADg&usg=AFQjCNGDh-fEkdc2B9jNGSCqK4sX-ZEVMw`

▶ Information on data marts in Business Intelligence is available at `http://www.yellowfinbi.com/YFForum-Whats-a-Data-Mart-?thread=92098`

Looking into SAP HANA features

This section explains the features of SAP HANA that make it so special when compared with other in-memory and traditional databases.

Getting ready

For every organization, information is required and acts as an asset to make decisions and run the business. Having the assets doesn't matter, but capitalizing on them remains of high priority. However, delivering this capability to everyone in the organization is impossible. The in-memory computing feature of SAP HANA is a disruptive force that offers speed and swiftness to power analytics at an exceptional performance level while remaining cost effective. To summarize, SAP HANA, built on Intel(R) Xeon(R) Processor 7500 Series, delivers the following features:

> ▸ **Speed and agility**: The business commanding for quick change is to create new demands for business and technology. All the data has to be made available to the business users; making sure that no delay occurs on the part of the enterprise data warehouse is critical.

> ▸ **Performance and cost**: Advances in hardware and software technologies have improved performance dramatically, without making a huge difference to the maintenance cost. This helps make new computing models.

How to do it...

Different scenarios faced by organizations and how SAP HANA features help organizations find a solution while making tough decisions are discussed here.

Alignment of business and IT

Business requirements are very dynamic and highly critical, and there is a need to ensure continuity. Business users and business analysts need to be empowered by having the flexibility to define their views on the information and the application, based on their look and feel, aesthetics, and requirements. The Information Technology Department should strive for business continuity, low redundancy, and the optimal reuse of the systems, information, resources, and infrastructure available.

More efficient data processing

The move to the SAP in-memory computing engine is a paradigm shift to an innovative foundation that can truly fulfill the promise of real-time analytics and business in the present and future.

Business analytic applications powered by technology

Technology has empowered business analytic applications, industry-specific solutions, and functional areas of businesses. Customers need the technological capabilities and empowerment of powerful technology to harness the full potential of data with ease, not only to enable but also to transform various aspects of the business.

The SAP in-memory computing engine, part of SAP HANA, delivers the following capabilities:

- A unified database with native support for row and columnar datastores, providing the RDBMS properties, such as atomicity, consistency, isolation, and durability (ACID)
- An interface that supports both SQL and **Multidimensional Expressions** (**MDX**)
- A combined information modeling design environment
- Views related to business information are stored in the data repository
- Data integration capabilities for accessing both SAP and non-SAP data sources
- An integrated LCM—lifecycle management capabilities for transporting and version management capabilities

The capabilities that are mentioned in the preceding list enable the SAP in-memory computing engine to support and process massive amounts of data from heterogeneous data sources in the enterprise; apply complex calculations that are necessary for decision makers to explore and analyze vast amounts of data; and derive actionable insights and information with faster response times, greater flexibility, and much less dependency on the IT team for decision-making.

Powerful analytic appliance – real-time insight

Business users and stakeholders of organizations can instantly analyze, explore, and access all of their transactional and analytical data in real time from virtually any data source. The data might be operational, analytical, tactical, or strategic in nature, however the in-memory technology allows users to access the previously mentioned types of data in a single snapshot.

External data can be easily integrated or added to analytical models of SAP HANA without going through any cumbersome processes to integrate data from sources of the entire organization.

How it works...

To outline some general distinctive features and design guidelines and show the key differentiators with respect to common, relational, SQL-based database management systems, the features described in this section represent the cornerstones of the philosophy behind the SAP HANA database.

A multi-engine query processing environment

In order to cope with the requirements of managing enterprise data with different characteristics in different ways, the SAP HANA database comprises a multi-engine query processing environment. In order to support the core features of enterprise applications, the SAP HANA database provides SQL-based access to relationally structured data with full transactional support. Since more and more applications require the enrichment and enhancement of classically structured data with semi-structured, unstructured, or text data, the SAP HANA database provides a text search engine in addition to its classical relational query engine.

The HANA database engine supports the joining of semistructured data to relations in the classical model, in addition to supporting direct entity extraction procedures on semi structured data. Finally, a graph engine, which is a GUI, natively provides the capability to run graph algorithms on networks of data entities to support business applications, such as supply chain optimization, production planning, and social network analyses.

Representation of application-specific business objects

In contrast to classical relational databases, the SAP HANA database is able to provide a deep understanding of the business objects used in the application layer. The SAP HANA database makes it possible to register the semantic models inside the database engine to push down more application semantics into the data management layer. In addition to registering semantically richer data structures (for example, OLAP cubes with measures and dimensions), SAP HANA also provides access to specific business logics implemented directly, deep inside the database engine. The SAP HANA Business Function Library summarizes those application procedures.

Development of current hardware innovations

Modern data management systems must consider current developments with respect to large amounts of available main memory, the number of cores per node, cluster configurations, and SSD/flash storage characteristics in order to efficiently leverage modern hardware resources and guarantee good query performance at affordable prices. The SAP HANA database is built from the ground up to execute in parallel and main-memory-centric environments. In particular, providing scalable parallelism is the overall design criteria for both the system and application levels.

Direct access to ERP

SAP HANA provides direct connectivity and access to transactional and operational data without disrupting the performance of SAP ERP. Organizations that require business continuity can easily synchronize into memory the key transactional tables that reside in SAP HANA in real time, making these tables easily accessible for business analysis.

Direct access to other (non-SAP) systems

SAP HANA can integrate and access any standard data source applicable. In scenarios where organizations require operational or transactional data from non-SAP systems or would like to expand on existing analytic models, any source of data can be used as the foundation for analytics in SAP HANA. Using the SAP BusinessObjects Data Services component, data can be loaded from non-SAP systems into SAP HANA. SAP Data Services is a strategic ETL tool in SAP for heterogeneous sources, data from different sources can be transformed, cleaned, and integrated. This enables us to load data into SAP HANA from different sources. SAP HANA provides an easy-to-use, rich graphical interface, enabling modeling experience to further increase the flexibility in use for business users. Using the semantically enriched information modeling layer of SAP HANA, information views can be created that transform the raw data into relevant and insightful analytical information which helps business users to consume data using SAP BusinessObjects reports, explorer views, and dashboards on the Web or handheld devices (iPad, Android devices, Blackberry, and so on).

There's more...

Apart from those that we have seen, let's see another feature of SAP HANA.

Leveraging BI capabilities

SAP HANA provides standard interfaces and connectivity to applications, operational systems, and business applications in the current IT landscape. This means that SAP HANA will not disrupt existing landscapes and complements them by connecting to their data sources, leveraging the current investments such as BI clients. The business intelligence and analytical capabilities of SAP BusinessObjects can leverage SAP HANA's in-memory feature as there exists SQL and MDX direct connectivity, and the views created in SAP HANA can be consumed in the SAP BusinessObjects reporting and analytical tools in an easy manner, giving business users a complete, wide range of capabilities for analytics and deriving insightful information. SAP HANA provides different possibilities for users, whether they prefer to use Excel or other tools and applications, via standard interfaces such as MDX or SQL.

Comparing BWA and SAP HANA

In this section, we will be covering the evolution of SAP HANA and its innovation process. SAP was one of the early pioneers in using in-memory technology as it has been highly consistent in improving the performance for gaining high data compression and achieving real-time analytics.

Evolution of SAP BWA and SAP HANA

TREX and SAP Enterprise Search were some of the first products to innovate and use the concepts of in-memory and column-based storage. Based on the strength of these products, SAP developed SAP NetWeaver BW Accelerator, which is an in-memory product mainly for performance optimization.

With SAP NetWeaver BW Accelerator established in the customer's IT enterprise landscape and market, SAP has consistently expanded its vision to continuously innovate to utilize this in-memory technology to benefit its customers. The vision was to respond to the business requirements for enterprises in combining OLTP and OLAP by removing the requirements of pre-aggregated, precalculated queries/indexes and other related features resulting in data latency and days or weeks in getting the business reports.

SAP's focus on business intelligence has led to the decision to combine the business intelligence functions from SAP BusinessObjects (after SAP's acquisition of Business Objects at the end of the year 2007) with the in-memory analytical engine of SAP NetWeaver BW Accelerator, creating an accelerated business intelligence solution called SAP BusinessObjects Explorer. With a focus on technology-agnostic solutions and heterogeneity, SAP then improvised SAP BusinessObjects Explorer by including data integration capabilities in SAP NetWeaver BW.

The innovative in-memory computing engine of SAP HANA is the next generation analytics technology. It complements today's SAP NetWeaver BW Accelerator with enhancements and additional functions, including the replication and acceleration of transactional data for real-time analytics. Customers can use SAP HANA as not only the technology, but also the platform for delivering accelerated analytical solutions. SAP HANA, currently strategic in-memory real-time analytics, is a solution offered by SAP.

How it works...

Now let us compare BWA and SAP HANA.

Comparison

BWA was specifically designed to accelerate BW queries by reducing the data acquisition time by storing copies of the InfoCube data in-memory. The purpose of SAP BWA is to improve the query performance of SAP NetWeaver BW. The SAP BW 7.0 release and later versions supports SAP BWA. In simple terms, SAP BWA is optimized for SAP BW primarily for performance improvisation.

SAP HANA is an in-memory appliance and platform for delivering high-performance analytics and applications and also real-time analytical solutions. SAP HANA is a full-featured in-memory database, and the data can be loaded into SAP HANA from SAP and non-SAP data sources and be consumed using SAP BusinessObjects frontend tools. SAP HANA also acts as an in-memory database that powers SAP NetWeaver BW 7.3 and later versions; SAP HANA can be used as accelerators also in implementing Sidecar scenarios and SOH—Business Suite on SAP HANA (CRM on HANA, SRM on HANA, and ERP on HANA). In this way, it is optimized and designed to dramatically improve the overall performance of SAP BW.

See also

- Learn more about BIA Engine at `http://wiki.sdn.sap.com/wiki/display/BI/BIA+Engine`

B
Architecture

The beauty of SAP HANA lies in its architecture. The way it is built makes it unique and very special compared to other databases. This appendix explains the architecture of SAP HANA, the different components, and their importance.

In this appendix, we will cover:

- Understanding the SAP HANA architecture
- Explaining IMCE and its components
- Storing data – row storage
- Storing data – column storage
- Understanding the persistence layer
- Understanding backup and recovery

Understanding the SAP HANA architecture

Enterprise application requirements have become more demanding—complex reports with high computation on huge volumes of transaction data and also business data of other formats (both structured and semi-structured). Data is being written or updated, and also read from the database in parallel. Thus, integration of both transactional and analytical data into single database is required. SAP HANA has evolved from here. Columnar storage exploits modern hardware and technology (multiple CPU cores, large main memory, and caches) to achieve the requirements of enterprise applications. Apart from this, it should also support procedural logic where certain tasks cannot be completed with simple SQL.

The SAP HANA database consists of several services (servers). The index server is the most important component of all the servers. Other servers are name server, preprocessor server, statistics server, and XS Engine:

- **Index server**: This server holds the actual data and engines for processing the data. When SQL or MDX is fired against the SAP HANA system in the case of authenticated sessions and transactions, an index server takes care of these commands and processes them.

- **Name server**: This server holds complete information about the system landscape. Name server is responsible for the topology of the SAP HANA system. In a distributed system, SAP HANA instances will be running on multiple hosts. In this kind of setup, the name server knows where the components are running and how data is spread on different servers.

- **Preprocessor server**: This server comes into the picture during text data analysis. Index server utilizes the capabilities of preprocessor server in text data analysis and searching. This helps to extract the information on which text search capabilities are based.

- **Statistics server**: This server helps to collect the data for the system monitor and helps you know the health of the SAP HANA system. The statistics server is responsible for collecting the data related to status, resource allocation/consumption, and performance of the SAP HANA system. Monitoring the status of various alert monitors requires the data collected by statistics server. This server also provides a history of measurement data for further analysis.

- **XS Engine**: The XS Engine allows external applications and application developers to access the SAP HANA system via the XS Engine clients, for example, a web browser accesses SAP HANA apps built by application developers via HTTP. Application developers build applications by using the XS Engine, and the users access the app via HTTP by using a web browser. The persistent model in the SAP HANA database is converted into a consumption model for clients to access it via HTTP. This allows an organization to host system services that are a part of the SAP HANA database (for example, Search service, a built-in web server that provides access to static content in the repository).

The following diagram shows the architecture of SAP HANA:

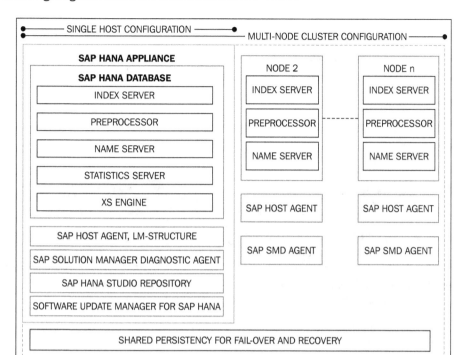

Let us continue learning about the different components:

- **SAP Host Agent**: According to the new approach from SAP, the SAP Host Agent should be installed on all machines that are related to the SAP landscape. It is used by **Adaptive Computing Controller** (**ACC**) to manage the system and **Software Update Manager** (**SUM**) for automatic updates.

- **LM-structure**: LM-structure for SAP HANA contains the information about current installation details. This information will be used by SUM during automatic updates.

- **SAP Solution Manager diagnostic agent**: This agent provides all the data to **SAP Solution Manager** (**SAP SOLMAN**) to monitor the SAP HANA system. After the SAP SOLMAN is integrated with the SAP HANA system, this agent provides information about the database at a glance, which includes the database state and general information about the system, such as alerts, CPU, or memory and disk usage.

- **SAP HANA Studio repository**: This helps the end users to update the SAP HANA studio to higher versions. The SAP HANA Studio repository is the code that does this process.

- **Software Update Manager for SAP HANA**: This helps in automatic updates of SAP HANA from the SAP Marketplace and patching the SAP host agent. It also allows distribution of the Studio repository to the end users.

For more information, refer to the following links:

- `http://help.sap.com/hana/SAP_HANA_Installation_Guide_en.pdf`
- SAP Note 1793303 at `https://websmp230.sap-ag.de/sap(bD1lbiZjPTAwMQ==)/bc/bsp/sno/ui_entry/entry.htm?param=69765F6D6F64653D3030312669765F7361706E6F7465735F6E756D626572 3D303030303137393333303326`
- SAP HANA Central note at `https://websmp230.sap-ag.de/sap(bD1lbiZjPTAwMQ==)/bc/bsp/sno/ui_entry/entry.htm?param=69765F6D6F64653D3030312669765F7361706E6F7465735F6E756D626572 3D303030303135313439363726`

Explaining IMCE and its components

The SAP **in-memory computing (IMCE) engine** (formerly **Business Analytic Engine** (**BAE**)) is the core engine for SAP's next generation high-performance, in-memory solutions. This is because it leverages technologies such as in-memory computing, columnar databases, **massively parallel processing** (**MPP**), and data compression to allow organizations to instantly explore and analyze large volumes of transactional and analytical data from across the enterprise in real time.

In-memory computing allows the processing of massive quantities of real-time data in the main memory of the server, providing immediate results from analyses and transactions. The SAP **in-memory computing database** delivers the following capabilities:

- In-memory computing functionality with native support for row and columnar datastores providing full **ACID** (**atomicity, consistency, isolation, and durability**) transactional capabilities
- Integrated lifecycle management capabilities and data integration capabilities to access SAP and non-SAP data sources
- SAP IMCE Studio that includes tools for data modeling, data and life cycle management, and data security

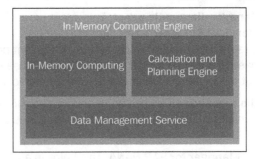

The SAP IMCE that resides at the heart of SAP HANA is an integrated database and calculation layer that allows the processing of massive quantities of real-time data in the main memory to provide immediate results from analysis and transactions. Like any standard database, the SAP IMCE not only supports industry standards such as SQL and MDX, but also incorporates a high-performance calculation engine that embeds procedural language support directly into the database kernel. This approach is designed to remove the need to read data from the database, process it, and then write data back to the database, that is, process the data near the database and return the results.

The IMCE is an in-memory, column-oriented database technology. It is a powerful calculation engine at the heart of SAP HANA. As data resides in the **Random Access Memory** (**RAM**), highly accelerated performance can be achieved compared to systems that read data from disks. The heart lies within the IMCE, which allows us to create and perform calculations on data. SAP IMCE Studio includes tools for data modeling activities, data and life cycle management, and also tools that are related to data security. The following diagram shows the complete architecture of SAP HANA, including IMCE and how it is connected to different components:

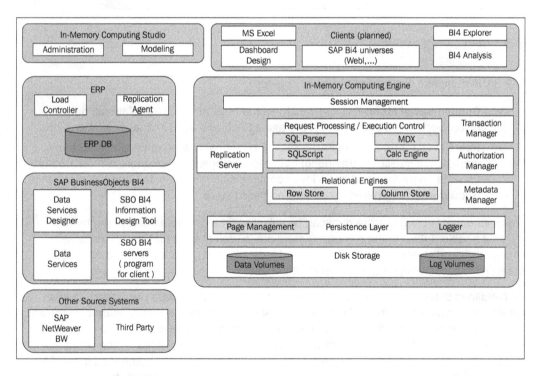

The following diagram shows the components of IMCE alone:

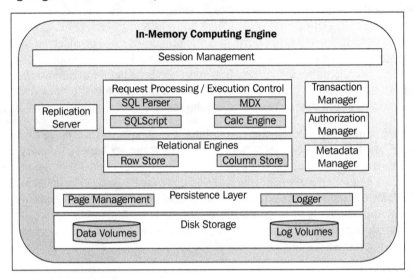

Further reading

SAP HANA database has the following two engines:

> ▶ **Column-based store**: This engine stores the huge amounts of relational data in column-optimized tables, which are aggregated and used in analytical operations.

> ▶ **Row-based store**: This engine stores the relational data in rows, similar to the storage mechanism of traditional database systems. The row store is more optimized for write operations and has a lower compression rate. Also, the query performance is lower when compared to the column-based store.

The engine that is used to store data can be selected on a per-table basis at the time of creating a table. Tables in the row-based store are loaded at start up time. In the case of column-based stores, tables can be either loaded at start up or on demand, that is, during normal operation of the SAP HANA database.

Both engines share a common persistence layer, which provides data persistency that is consistent across both engines. Like a traditional database, we have page management and logging in SAP HANA. The changes made to the in-memory database pages are persisted through savepoints. These savepoints are written to those data volumes on the persistent storage for which the storage medium is hard drives. All transactions committed in the SAP HANA database are stored/saved/referenced by the logger of the persistency layer in a log entry written to the log volumes on the persistent storage. To get high I/O performance and low latency, log volumes use the flash technology storage.

The relational engines can be accessed through a variety of interfaces. The SAP HANA database supports SQL (JDBC/ODBC), MDX (ODBO), and BICS (SQLDBC). The calculation engine performs all the calculations in the database. No data moves into the application layer until calculations are completed. It also contains the business functions library that is called by applications to perform calculations based on the business rules and logic. The SAP HANA-specific SQL script language is an extension of SQL that can be used to push down data-intensive application logic into the SAP HANA database for specific requirements.

Session management

This component creates and manages sessions and connections for the database clients. When a session is created, a set of parameters are maintained in the backend by the system. These parameters include auto-commit settings and the current transaction isolation level. After establishing a session, database clients communicate with the SAP HANA database using SQL statements. SAP HANA database treats all the statements as transactions while processing them. Each new session created will be assigned to a new transaction.

Transaction manager

The transaction manager is the component that coordinates database transactions, takes care of controlling transaction isolation, and keeps track of running and closed transactions. The transaction manager informs the involved storage engines about the running or closed transactions, so that they can execute necessary actions when a transaction is committed or rolled back. The transaction manager cooperates with the persistence layer to achieve atomic and durable transactions.

Atomicity is one of the ACID transaction properties. In an atomic transaction, when a series of database operations are present, either all occur or nothing occurs. A guarantee of atomicity prevents updates to the database occurring only partially, which can cause greater problems than rejecting the whole series outright.

Durability guarantees the transactions that have committed will survive permanently. For example, if a flight booking software reports that a seat has successfully been booked, then the seat will remain booked even if the system crashes.

The client requests are analyzed and executed by a set of components summarized as request processing and execution control. The client requests are analyzed by a request parser, and then it is dispatched to the responsible component. The transaction control statements are forwarded to the transaction manager. The data definition statements are sent to the metadata manager. The object invocations are dispatched to the object store. The data manipulation statements are sent to the optimizer, which creates an optimized execution plan that is given to the execution layer.

The SAP HANA database also has built-in support for domain-specific models (such as for financial planning domain) and it offers scripting capabilities that allow application-specific calculations to run inside the database. It has its own scripting language named **SQLScript** that is designed to enable optimizations and parallelization. This SQLScript is based on side-effect free functions that operate on tables by using SQL queries for set processing.

The SAP HANA database also contains a component called the planning engine that allows financial planning applications to execute basic planning operations in the database layer. For example, while applying filters/transformations, a new version of a dataset will be created as a copy of an existing one. An example of planning operation is the disaggregation operation. In this operation, the target values from higher to lower aggregation levels are distributed based on a distribution function.

Metadata manager

Metadata manager helps to access metadata. SAP HANA database's metadata consists of a variety of objects, such as definitions of tables, views and indexes, SQLScript function definitions, and object store metadata. All these types of metadata are stored in one common catalog for all the SAP HANA database stores. Metadata is stored in tables in the row store. The SAP HANA features such as transaction support and **multi-version concurrency control** (**MVCC**) are also used for metadata management. Central metadata is shared across the servers in the case of a distributed database systems. The background mechanism of metadata storage and sharing is hidden from the components that use the metadata manager.

As row-based tables and columnar tables can be combined in one SQL statement, both the row and column engines must be able to consume the intermediate results. The main difference between the two engines is the way they process data: the row store operators process data in a row-at-a-time fashion, whereas column store operations (such as scan and aggregate) require the entire column to be available in contiguous memory locations. To exchange intermediate results created by each other, the row store provides results to the column store. The result materializes as complete rows in the memory, while the column store can expose results using the iterators interface needed by the row store.

Persistence layer

The persistence layer is responsible for durability and atomicity of transactions. The persistent layer ensures that the database is restored to the most recent committed state after a restart, and makes sure that transactions are either completely executed or completely rolled back. To achieve this in an efficient way, the persistence layer uses a combination of write-ahead logs, shadow paging, and savepoints. Moreover, the persistence layer also offers interfaces for writing and reading data. It also contains SAP HANA's logger that manages the transaction log.

Authorization manager

The authorization manager is invoked by other SAP HANA database components to check the required privileges for users to execute the requested operations. Privileges to other users or roles can be granted. A privilege grants the right to perform a specified operation (such as create, update, select, and execute data manipulation languages) on a specified object such as a table, view, and SQLScript function. Analytic privileges represent filters or hierarchy, and they drill down limitations for analytic queries. Analytic privileges such as granting access to values with a certain combination of dimension attributes are supported in SAP HANA. Users are authenticated either by the SAP HANA database itself (log in with username and password), or authentication can be delegated to external authentication providers third-party such as an LDAP directory.

For more information, you can refer to the SAP HANA at the following links:

- `http://searchbusinessanalytics.techtarget.com/definition/in-memory-analytics`

- `http://www.sap.com/india/pc/tech/in-memory-computing-hana.html`

- `http://scn.sap.com/people/vitaliy.rudnytskiy/blog/2011/03/22/time-to-update-your-sap-hana-vocabulary`

In-Memory Computing

`http://scn.sap.com/people/vitaliy.rudnytskiy/blog/2011/03/22/time-to-update-your-sap-hana-vocabulary`

Storing data – row storage

As seen in the architectural diagram of SAP HANA IMCE, there are two relational engines in the heart of the IMCE. These relational engines are in-memory, meaning that their primary data persistence is based in RAM. The row store stores the data in rows, and in this respect, it behaves like a traditional database—except that the data always resides in RAM. The row store engine is highly optimized for write operations and is interfaced from the calculation/execution layer. All the operations on the row tables will be processed by this row engine. When a query is fired on to the SAP HANA database, the optimizer decides in which engine the query has to be executed. For example, there may be some functions that OLAP engine doesn't support, but the row engine does. In that case, the optimizer sends all the data to the row engine and gets the task done. This may be more expensive as the column data has to be converted to row data before it is processed by row engine. One such example is non equi join. Non equi joins will be executed by the row engine only as this is not supported by the column engine.

Now, let us see the internal architecture of the SAP HANA row store engine in the following diagram:

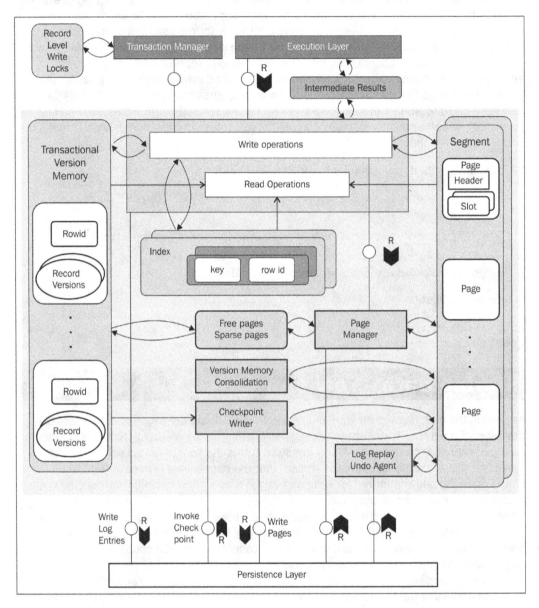

The main functions of the different components are explained as follows:

- ▶ **Transactional Version Memory**: This memory sections holds the temporary version of data. All the recent versions of changed records are maintained in this section. This data is required by MVCC. For concurrency control, SAP HANA implements the classic MVCC principle to provide concurrent access to the database. Data reading and writing will happen in parallel from database. When the data is being written and some users are reading the same data, there are fair chances that the data is inconsistent. To avoid this, techniques such as locking and MVCC are implemented.

  Locking is an effective way of handling concurrency problem, but takes lot of time. However, MVCC is very effective in handling the latest versions of data. When a query hits the database, the data at that instant of time is displayed. The changes made will not be reflected in the results until the transaction is committed to the database.

  When there is a new set of data to be updated, MVCC will not update the old data set. Instead, it marks the old data as outdated and writes a new set of data elsewhere. In this process, there will be many versions of data stored—only one being the latest. Hence, a considerable amount of memory is required to maintain these data versions. MVCC in combination with a time-travel mechanism allows temporal queries inside the relational engine.

- ▶ **Segments**: Segments contain the actual data in the form of pages. All the data in the row-store tables are stored in segments, in the form of pages. The concept of linked list is used in storing the memory pages. Linked list is one of the fundamental data structures. The SAP HANA database uses the same concept. The row store tables are linked lists of memory pages. Pages are grouped in segments. The typical size of each page is 16 KB.

- ▶ **Page Manager**: Page Manager is responsible for memory allocation. It also keeps track of the used pages and the free pages available.

- ▶ **Version Memory Consolidation**: As discussed earlier, different versions of the data are stored in the transactional version memory and MVCC takes care of the data consistency. When a transaction is committed, it has to be stored in a database table, a row table in this case. Version Memory Consolidation takes care of this activity. The recent versions of the changed records are moved from the transaction version memory to the persistent segment on commit-ID basis. After moving the recent version to the persistent segment, all the temporary data and the different versions created by MVCC have to be cleared from the transaction version memory for effective utilization of memory. This activity is also taken care of by Version Memory Consolidation. Hence, Version Memory Consolidation can be considered as garbage collector for MVCC.

- ▶ **Persistence Layer**: Persistence Layer is used for writing purposes. It is called in log write operations and checkpoints. All the database logs are maintained by the log replay/undo agent. After the data has been reloaded into the data area of database, it will replay the log from the log backups and the log area. The database will be back online only after these actions are completed.

The redo log information is located in the log backup and in the log area of the database. The recovery process takes care of checking log positions in the data backup after the data area has been restored. In order to replay the logs, the log position must be available either in the log backups or the log area. Also, the system should find the offset on the log. If the backup being used for recovery is not the latest one, we must ensure that the offset needed for the backups is available in the log backups or the log area. Unless the required offset is present, log replay cannot be performed.

During recovery, if the system cannot find the log offset in the log area, we see an error message **log and data must be compatible**. In this error situation, we must use the clear log option during to get the system online again. Any logs in the log area are ignored during the log replay phase. Even if the replay of the log area is not performed, the system ends up in a consistent data state. The data area holds all the undo log information, and it is reloaded into the area during recovery. The replication server won't have a restart point if the log replay has not taken place. When this situation occurs, it is essential to refer to the replication server documentation for information on how to solve this problem.

If we perform a recovery without implicit log replay, the log area is formatted. The log backups are replayed, but not the logs in the log area. In this situation, the .ini files can be recovered. On the other hand, their recovery is not important. If the .ini files are recovered, parameter changes made after the backup will not be recovered; therefore they are lost.

When we use the clear log option, the following actions will be performed:

▶ The data changes made after the back up will be lost; as the log entries get cleared from the system, there is no more information available to perform redo

▶ The transactions that are not yet committed in the backup area will be rolled back (undo)

Only when the log replay of the log area cannot take place, the clear log option has to be used as an exception.

The following are examples of situations where the log replay may not be possible:

▶ When the log area is corrupted and the log information is no longer available

▶ A log backup is missing, which links the latest available log backup to the log area

▶ While performing a disaster recovery if the log available in the log backups and the log in the log area are not compatible

Let us complete our learning about all the components of the row store engine:

▶ **Write Operations**: When there are any write operations, they mainly go to the Transaction Version Memory. Here, all the versions are maintained by MVCC and finally written to Persisted Segment. The *Insert* operation also writes the data to Persisted Segment.

- ▸ **Persisted Segment**: Persisted Segment contains data that is used in ongoing active transactions and data that has been committed before any active transaction was started.

- ▸ **Index**: Each row-store table has a primary index. ROW ID is a number that specifies the memory segment and page for each record. Primary index maps Primary Key of the table to ROW ID. ROW ID contains the segment address and the offset. To locate a record, combination of segment address and segment offset is used. The formula becomes Segment Address + Segment Offset. The memory page for a table record can be obtained. A structure called ROW ID contains the segment and the page for the record. The page can then be searched for the records based on Primary Key. As mentioned earlier, ROW ID is a part of the primary index of the table.

Indices are never persistent. They are always stored in the memory only. When tables are loaded into the memory on system start up, indices for all the row tables are filled. They are never stored permanently.

We can create secondary indices if required. It is better to go with row storage in the following situations:

- ▸ It is recommended when the tables contain a low volume of data

- ▸ It is used when the application request has to access the entire row

- ▸ It is used when the data has to be processed record by record

For more information, refer to the following link:

```
http://scn.sap.com/community/developer-center/hana/blog/2012/08/16/
in-a-relationship-with-hana--part-3
```

Storing data – column storage

Having learned about the row store engine of SAP HANA, now let us learn about the column store engine. Data will be stored in RAM, similar to the row store engine. The concept of column storage has emerged from **Text Retrieval and Extraction** (**TREX**). This technology was further developed into a full relational column-based datastore. Compression works well with columns and can speed up operations on columns up to a factor of 10. Column storage is optimized for high performance of a read operation. There are two types of indices for column store table for each column: a main storage and a delta storage. For write operations, the delta storage is optimized. The main storage is optimized in terms of the read performance and memory consumption. Performance issues when loading directly to compressed columns can be addressed by the delta tables.

The architecture of a column store is shown in the following diagram:

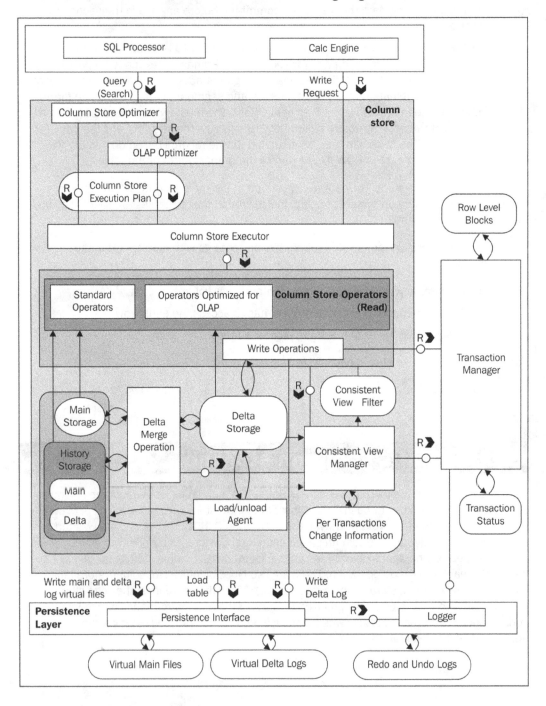

The components of the column engine are explained as follows:

- **Optimizer and Executor**: Optimizer gets the logical execution plan from SQL Parser or Calc engine as input, and generates the optimized physical execution plan based on the database statistics. The best plan for accessing row or column stores will be determined by the database optimizer. Executor basically executes the physical execution plan to access the row and column stores, and also processes all the intermediate results.

- **Main Storage**: Data is highly compressed and stored in the main storage. Being compressed and stored in column storage, data is read very fast.

- **Delta Storage**: Delta storage is designed for fast writing operation. When there is an update operation to be performed, a new entry is added into the delta storage.

- **Delta Merge**: Write operations are only performed on the delta storage. The database is transferred to the main storage in order to transform the data into a format that is optimized in terms of memory consumption and read performance. This is accomplished by a process called delta merge. The following section is intended to give a better understanding of how this happens and when.

The delta merge process

The following diagram describes the different states of a merge process, which objects are involved, and how they are accessed.

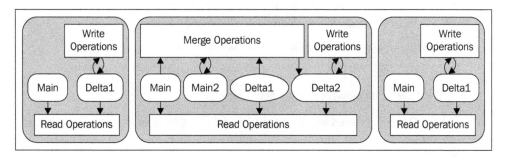

The following operations are performed for the merge process:

- **Before the merge operation**: All the write operations go to the storage **Delta1**, and the read operations read from the storages **Main1** and Delta1.

- **During the merge operation**: When the merge operation is in progress, all the changes go into the second delta storage **Delta2**. The read operations continue from the original main storage (Main1) and from both the delta storage (Delta1 and Delta2). The uncommitted changes from Delta1 are copied to Delta2. The committed entries in Delta1 and content of Main1 are merged into the new main storage, that is, **Main2**.

- **After the merge operation**: Main1 and Delta1 storages are deleted after the merge operation is complete.

Consistent view manager and transaction manager

The consistent view manager creates a consistent view throughout data for the moment in time when the query hits the system. Isolation of concurrent transactions is enforced by a central transaction manager, maintaining information about all write transactions and the consistent view manager deciding on visibility of records per table. A so-called transaction token is generated by the transaction manager for each transaction, encoding which transactions are open, and is committed at the point in time when the transaction has started. The transaction token holds all the information needed to construct the consistent view for a transaction or a statement. It is passed as additional context information to all the operations and engines that are involved in the execution of a statement.

It is better to go with column storage under the following situations:

- Recommended when the tables contain huge volumes of data
- Used when lot of aggregations need to be done on the tables
- Used when the tables have huge number of columns
- Used when the table has to be searched based on the values of few columns

The main advantages with column storage are

- Number of cache cycles will be reduced and this will help to retrieve the data at a faster rate
- Supports parallel processing

For more information, refer the following links:

- http://scn.sap.com/people/neha.singla/blog/2012/02/20/column-store-in-sap-hana
- http://scn.sap.com/community/developer-center/hana/blog/2013/05/21/a-brief-comparison-of-sap-iq-and-hana-column-store-databases

Understanding the persistence layer

SAP HANA's persistence layer manages logging of all the transactions in order to provide standard backup and restore functions. Both the row stores and column stores interact with the persistence layer. It offers regular savepoints, and also logging of all database transaction since the last savepoint.

The persistence layer is responsible for the durability and atomicity of transactions. The persistence layer manages both data and log volumes on the disk, and also provides interfaces to read and write data that is leveraged by all the storage engines. This layer is built based on the persistency layer of MaxDB, SAP's traditional relational database. The persistency layer guarantees that the database is restored to the most recent committed state after a restart, and these transactions are either completely executed or completely rolled back. To accomplish this efficiently, it uses a blend of write-ahead logs, shadow paging, and savepoints.

To enable scalability in terms of data volumes and the number of application requests, the SAP HANA database supports scale-up and scale-out. Keeping data in the main memory brings up the question of what will happen in the case of a loss of power.

In database technology, atomicity, consistency, isolation, and durability (ACID) are a set of requirements that guarantees that the database transactions are processed reliably:

- A transaction has to be atomic. This means the transaction should be either executed completely or fail completely. The database state should be unchanged, and the entire transaction has to fail if a part of it fails.

- Consistency of a database must be unspoiled by the transactions that it performs.

- Isolation ensures that all transactions are independent.

- Durability means that there is no change in the state of a transaction, that is, a transaction will remain committed after it has been committed.

While the first three requirements are not affected by the in-memory database concepts, durability is the lone requirement that cannot be met by storing data in the main memory. The main memory is a volatile storage; its content will be cleared when power is switched off. To make data persistent, non-volatile storage (such as hard drives, SSD, or flash devices) have to be used.

Further reading

The storage used by a database to store data is divided into pages. When data changes occur due to transactions, the changed pages are marked and written to the non-volatile storage at regular intervals. In addition to this, all changes made by the transactions are captured by database log. All the committed transactions generate a log entry, and these are written to non-volatile storage. This confirms that all transactions are stored permanently. The following diagram illustrates this using the example of SAP HANA. All the changed pages are saved in the form of savepoints, which are asynchronously written to persistent storage at regular intervals (by default, every five minutes). The log is written synchronously, that is, transaction does not return before the corresponding log entry that has been written to the persistent storage.

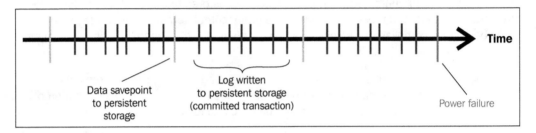

After a power failure, the database can be restarted like a disk-based database. Database pages from the savepoints are restored, and then the database logs are applied (rolled forward) to restore the changes that were not captured in the savepoints. This ensures that the database can be restored in the memory to exactly the same state as it was before the power failure.

The SAP in-memory database holds the bulk of its data in the memory for maximum performance. It still depends on persistent storage to provide a fallback in case of failure. The log captures all changes done by the database transactions (redo logs).

Data and undo log information (parts of data) are automatically saved to the disk at regular savepoints. The log is also saved to the disk continuously and synchronously after each commit of a database transaction (waiting for the end of a disk write operation).

The database can be restarted after a power failure, just like a disk-based database:

- ▶ The system is normally restarted (*lazy* reloading of tables to keep the restart time short)
- ▶ The system returns to its last consistent state (by replaying the redo log since the last savepoint)

For more information, refer to the following link:

```
http://scn.sap.com/community/developer-center/hana/blog/2012/08/14/
in-a-relationship-with-hana--part-2
```

Understanding backup and recovery

In the SAP HANA database, during normal operation, data is automatically saved to the disk at regular savepoints. Furthermore, the log captures all the data changes. After each committed database transaction, the log is saved from the memory to the disk. When there is a power failure, the database can be restarted like any disk-based database, and it returns to its last consistent state by replaying the log since the last savepoint.

The backups are required for the following reasons:

- ▸ To protect against disk failures
- ▸ To make it possible to reset the database to an earlier point in time

Backups are carried out while the database is running and users can continue to work normally. The impact on system performance is negligible.

SAP HANA is an in-memory database or a database that stores its database tables in the main memory RAM. RAM is the fastest possible data storage media available as of today; however, it is volatile. During power loss, the data bits on the chip are erased or lost.

In order to avoid data loss, SAP HANA encompasses regular savepoints using two persistent storage volumes, that is, database logging or redo logging. With the combination of both redo logging and in-memory data savepoints, the system is fully capable of recovering from a sudden power failure.

The administration console of the SAP HANA studio provides a one-stop support environment for different activities such as system monitoring, back up and recovery, and user provisioning. The entire payload data from all the server nodes of the SAP HANA database instance are backed up as soon as the data area is backed up. This principle applies for both single-host and multihost environments.

During a log back up, the payload of the log segments is copied from the log area to the service-specific log backup files. Back up and recovery always applies to the entire database. It is not possible to back up or recover individual database objects. While performing a backup of the SAP HANA system, all the objects such as database tables, information models (that is, views and undo logs), information views, and metadata are all saved to a configurable persistent disk location. In the summary, all of the data and code that are stored in SAP HANA will be taken as a back up which is available at the specified path.

By default, the SAP HANA system creates log file backup for every 15 minutes (900 seconds), or when the standard log segments become full.

In case of scenarios of data center failures due to accidents such as fire, power outages, natural calamities such as earthquakes, or due to hardware failures such as the failure of any node, SAP HANA supports a hot-standby concept using synchronous mirroring with a redundant data center concept. This includes redundant SAP HANA databases also.

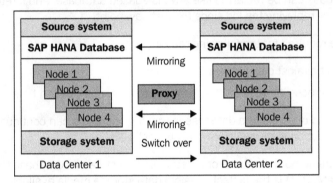

In addition, the cold-standby concept uses a standby system within one SAP HANA landscape, where the failover is triggered automatically. SAP HANA is an ACID-compliant database supporting atomicity, consistency, isolation, and durability of transactions.

In addition to recovery for **Online Analytical Processing** (**OLAP**), SAP HANA also provides transactional recovery for **Online Transactional Processing** (**OLTP**) through the administrative console in the SAP HANA studio.

The currently supported processes are given as follows:

- ► Recovery to last data backup
- ► Recovery to last and older (previous) data backup
- ► Recovery to last state before crash
- ► Point-in-time recovery

User provisioning is supported with role-based security, authentication, and analysis authorization using analytic privileges, which enables security for analytical objects based on a set of attribute values.

The administration console in SAP HANA Studio enables the version control mechanism for models of SAP HANA and SAP Data Services. SAP HANA can run in a single production landscape if the initial use case scenario is not business critical and the data load performance for the initial load is acceptable to reload the data. However, it is always recommended to align the SLT and SAP Data Services environment with the existing source system landscapes. When it comes to enterprise-grade business supporting mode of environment, SAP HANA needs to run in the standard landscape, that is, SAP development, quality assurance and staging, and production environments.

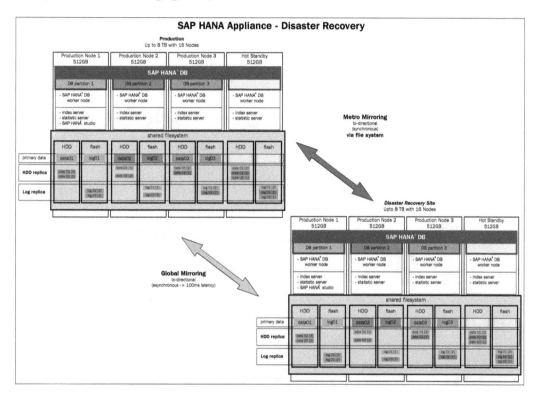

For scale-up scalability, all algorithms and data structures are designed to work on large multi-core architectures, especially focusing on the cache-aware data structures and code fragments. For scale-out scalability, the SAP HANA database is designed to run on a cluster of individual machines. This allows the distribution of data and query processing across multiple nodes. The scalability features of the SAP HANA database are heavily based on the proven technology of the SAP BWA product.

Also, refer to SAP Note: 1642148

Applications Powered by SAP HANA

In this appendix, we will cover:

- ▶ Introducing flavors on top of SAP HANA
- ▶ Introducing SAP NetWeaver BW powered by SAP HANA
- ▶ Introducing SAP Business Suite on SAP HANA

Introduction

SAP has been very predominant in the world of providing business applications for a long time. Now it has come up with few more applications powered by SAP HANA.

So far in this cookbook, we have seen that data-warehouse solutions are built in SAP HANA by staging data and creating models. But SAP HANA being an in-memory database, can power other applications by serving as a database. In this appendix, we will see how several applications are powered by SAP HANA, and how SAP HANA is different from other databases in supporting these applications.

Introducing flavors on top of SAP HANA

Applications on top of SAP HANA are being delivered by SAP to provide real-time insights on data. Applications require a database to store data. This is accomplished by SAP HANA. This section gives you an introduction to the applications available on top of SAP HANA.

How it works...

When applications are powered by SAP HANA, HANA acts as a database. The following points tell us how applications on SAP HANA work and their capabilities:

- ▶ Applications powered by SAP HANA are a new set of innovative applications that leverage the in-memory capabilities of SAP HANA. With these applications, customers are privileged to:
    - ❑ Perform analysis on Big Data by joining and calculating data like never before
    - ❑ Provide predictive and simulation capabilities
    - ❑ Perform analytics on transactions
    - ❑ Leverage the HTML5 capabilities and provide a better experience to users
- ▶ Applications powered by SAP HANA can be deployed in risk-free mode.

See also

- ▶ Several solutions powered by SAP HANA are available at `http://www54.sap.com/pc/tech/in-memory-computing-hana/software/applications/overview.html`

Introducing SAP NetWeaver BW powered by SAP HANA

In this section of the book, we will see how SAP HANA acts as a database for SAP BW.

Getting ready

With SAP HANA being an in-memory database, it works in a similar way to other traditional databases with regards to administration, and from a technical point of view.

How to do it...

SAP HANA acts as a database in the case of BW on HANA. There are three options to deploy SAP BW on HANA:

- ▶ **Fresh installation of BW on HANA**: In this option, we create a new BW instance and connect to the SAP HANA database. This is the easiest option of the three.

- **Upgrade the existing BW system**: In this option, we first upgrade the existing BW system to a minimum 7.3 SPS5. Then we change the underlying traditional disk-based relational database to the new in-memory database, the SAP HANA system.

- **System copy with BW on HANA**: In this method, we copy the running production BW system to a new system while keeping the production system running on existing traditional databases. Then, we migrate the newly copied BW system to the SAP HANA database so that downtime in the production environment can be reduced. Post-copy automation steps are followed to shorten the migration process. We can also have both the existing production BW system and the newly copied BW on the HANA system connected to the same ERP system. This can be accomplished by delta queue cloning and synchronization on the production systems.

How it works...

The SAP HANA appliance software with the SAP HANA database is preinstalled by the hardware vendor, certified by SAP on a validated hardware running a specific operating system. This HANA DB is installed on a separate server from the SAP NetWeaver BW system. The versions supported are SAP NetWeaver BW 7.3, SAP HANA SPS3, or higher versions. It is recommended by SAP to apply the latest available version.

During the process of setting up the SAP NetWeaver BW system, the ABAP schema and the data are loaded remotely into the SAP HANA database.

If we upgrade SAP NetWeaver BW on SAP HANA from SAP NetWeaver 7.3 to EhP1 for SAPNetWeaver 7.3, we have to first update the SAP HANA database to SP4 before upgrading the SAPNetWeaver system.

The following are the releases that SAP NW BW can run with:

- SAP NetWeaver 7.3 SPS 05 or higher running on SAP HANA SPS 03 or higher

- SAP EhP1 for SAP NetWeaver 7.3 SPS 04 or higher running on SAP HANA SPS 04 or higher

These are the benefits that can be harnessed by using SAP HANA as a database for SAP NetWeaver BW. We can also benefit from improved performance, as well as from the simplified administration and infrastructure created:

- Compared to SAP NetWeaver BWA, the query performance will be equal to or better than using BW on HANA.

- Complex analysis and planning scenarios with high data volume, unpredictable query types, complex calculations, and high query frequency can be achieved with a high degree of efficiency as in-memory feature supports very high efficiency to read operations. In addition, the query performance on the DataStore objects is comparable to the performance of InfoCubes.

▶ The loading process in SAP HANA-optimized data-warehouse objects can be processed with high efficiency.

▶ The SAP HANA database combines features of both the traditional database and SAP NetWeaver BWA, which helps to reduce costs for the required infrastructure setup. The same applies to the administration tools; we will require only a single set of administration tools, whereas we will require separate administration tools if we are using a database and SAP BWA separately. Similarly, a single set of tools will be enough for other activities such as monitoring, back up, and restore.

▶ Data modeling is simplified. For example, using SAP HANA-optimized objects means that it is not necessary to load the objects to a BWA index. Also, aggregates are not necessary when using the SAP HANA database. The column-based database architecture enables easier remodeling, for example, it allows us to delete characteristics from an InfoCube that still contains data.

▶ Furthermore, with improved query performance on DataStore objects, loading data from a DataStore object into a downstream InfoCube can become unnecessary if the InfoCube is only created to improve query performance. With its significant compression rate, the column-based storage ensures that less data needs to be materialized. The same column-based storage is used for all InfoProviders that save data as well as for the **Persistent Staging Area** (**PSA**).

See also

▶ User guides for SAP NetWeaver BW 7.3 powered by SAP HANA are available at:

  ❑ `http://www.sdn.sap.com/irj/scn/go/portal/prtroot/docs/`
    `library/uuid/e0b3f238-4ca0-3010-98ab-8826059a310c?QuickL`
    `ink=index&overridelayout=true&58695023067368`

  ❑ `http://help.sap.com/nw731bwhana`

Introducing SAP Business Suite on SAP HANA

SAP HANA is a game changing innovative database from SAP. This section is a brief introduction on how SAP ERP can be powered by SAP HANA.

How it works...

SAP HANA is a powerful in-memory technology addressing all concerns related to growing volumes of data. SAP HANA provides real-time analytics despite the fact that it simplifies existing IT landscapes. Customers will have the option to deploy models at a lower cost and with rapid innovation.

SAP HANA represents the fastest growing product in SAP's history. SAP Business Suite is a wide-ranging family of applications designed to work together to help run a business effectively and efficiently. From all over the world, more than 40,000 customers have invested in the SAP Business Suite software, and expect SAP to protect and add value to their investments. This is the reason SAP has delivered yet another SAP Business Suite application powered by SAP HANA, which has become the next generation platform. SAP HANA helps SAP to provide a modern suite of applications unifying analytics and transactions into a single in-memory platform.

Customers can now leverage the suite to rethink their business processes as required with embedded intelligence in the transactions. Besides combining analytics and transactions into a single system, the suite also enables the planning, execution, reporting, and analysis of data across end-to-end business processes in real time.

The SAP HANA platform provides the base to dramatically increase the performance of SAP Business Suite applications now and continue to innovate without disruption on an open platform.

SAP Business Suite powered by SAP HANA can help customers simplify IT by bringing together analytics and transactions for a reduced total cost of the ownership. As SAP HANA provides the unique ability to deal effectively with both transactional and analytical jobs, SAP Business Suite powered by SAP HANA can help customers achieve dramatic simplification of their IT landscape. In this context, SAP HANA can be used as a primary database for SAP Business Suite applications. There is no need for any replication of data since the same database is used for both analytical and transactional needs.

SAP Business Suite powered by SAP HANA allows access for everyone to any granularity holding complete transactional system data. The system also has the ability to perform predictive analysis and handle structured and unstructured data. All these operations can be performed in resource-intensive operations, in the real-time mode. The SAP HANA platform provides the foundation for customers to dramatically increase the performance of their SAP Business Suite applications now and continue to innovate without disruption by leveraging a new generation of real-time applications natively built on the platform.

SAP Business Suite applications using SAP HANA as the only database include SAP CRM, SAP ERP, and SAP SCM. These can fully run on top of SAP HANA in a unified fashion. This first wave of innovation from SAP provides optimizations for 23 business value scenarios across key lines of business (finance, service, sales, marketing, HR, procurement, and so on) and also includes more than 400 reports to achieve an unprecedented performance with SAP HANA in the context of the industry.

See also

▶ The following links tell you more about SAP ERP:

- ❏ https://proddps.hana.ondemand.com/dps/d/previe
  w/4bd269fe8b7b43e78c9fd1aca09f2096/2.0/en-US/
  d62e56e8ac5840f2b198c0c905892407.html

- ❏ http://www.saphana.com/docs/DOC-4042

- ❏ https://cookbook.experiencesaphana.com/crm/

Index

A

Administration Console perspective
about **9,** 15, 16
alerts 20
Configuration tab 19, 21
diagnosis files 21
Overview tab 19
performance related process 20
redistribution operations 19
services category 19
System, adding 16-19
System Information tab 21
Trace Configuration 22
Volumes tab 20
Administration option 12
aggregation 100
analytic privileges
about 203
creating 195-200
URL 200
analytic views
creating 90-93
appliance solution 216
application layer 210
atomic transaction 237
attribute views
creating 85-88
creating, steps for 87
types 86
attribute views, types
copy from 86
derived 86
standard 86
time 86

B

backup 249
bottlenecks 208
Business Analytic Engine (BAE) 234
Business Information Warehouse (BW) 70
business layer. *See also* **application layer**
business layer
creating 134-136

C

Calculation Engine (CE) 104
calculation views
creating 94, 95
creating, GUI used 95-104
creating, SQLScript used 104-109
CE_AGGREGATION 105
CE_CALC 105
CE_CALC_VIEW 104
CE_COLUMN_TABLE 104
CE_CONVERSION 105
CE functions
used, for creating calculation view 107, 108
CE_JOIN 104
CE_JOIN_VIEW 104
CE_LEFT_OUTER_JOIN 105

A

authentication
methods 200, 201
authorization manager 239
auto documentation
about 110
model details 111
model list 112

Central Management Console (CMC) 125
CE_OLAP_VIEW 104
CE_PROJECTION 105
CE_RIGHT_OUTER 105
CE_UNION_ALL 105
clickstreams 208
clients
  URL 123
column 181
column-based store engine 236
configuration, DXC 70, 71
configuration, Import Server 59
configuration, Sybase replication 76-78
Configuration tab 21
consistent view manager 246
control module 53
currency conversion
  about 172-174
  URL 174

D

dashboard
  URL 153
data
  access, restricting 195-200
  broadness 211
  column storage 243-245
  depth 211
  retrieval speed 212
  row storage 239-243
  simplicity 212
database layer 211
data cleansing, Information composer
  values, changing 115
  values, merging 114
data flow
  creating 66
  designing 67
  validating 68
data foundation
  about **186**
  creating 132-134
data, information composer
  cleansing 114

  loading 113, 114
  saving, in SAP HANA 115
  source, selecting 113, 114
  uploading 113
data, loading. *See* **data provisioning**
data provisioning
  about 25
  DXC, using for 70, 72
  from flat files 31-40
  methods 26
  SAP Data Services, using for 55, 68, 69
  SLT, used for 41, 51-54
  strategic considerations 28
  Sybase replication, using 75, 81, 82
  technical considerations 28
data replication
  about 42-50
  architecture 81
datastore
  creating, for SAP HANA system 64
  creating, in SAP Data Services 56, 57
  data flow, creating 66
  data flow, designing 67
  data flow, validating 68
  job, creating 65
  job, executing 68
  project, creating 64
  project, saving 68
  workflow, creating 66
DataStore Object (DSO) 70
Debug perspective 9
decision tables
  creating 185-188
  URL 188
delta merge process 245, 246
depth of data 211
derived from table 181
direct 181
Direct Extractor Connection (DXC)
  about 70
  configuring 70-72
  deployment option 73
  implementing, consideration 74
  using, for data provisioning 70, 72

E

Eclipse perspectives
  about 8
  Administration Console 9
  Debug 9
  Lifecycle Management 9
  Modeler 8
  SAP HANA Development 8
Enterprise HANA
  about 216
  technical requisites 217
ExpressConnect for HANA (ECH) 76

F

field mapping 36-40
filters
  creating 182, 183
Find System option 14
Find Table option 14
flat files
  data provisioning from 31-40
full, join type 88

G

GRANT statement 194
GUI
  used, for calculation view 95-100

H

hardware
  innovations 211
hierarchies
  creating 174
  leveled hierarchy 174
  parent-child hierarchy 176
  URL 177
**High-Performance Analytic
    Appliance (HANA) 205**

I

IMCE
  about 234, 235
  capabilities 234

Import Server
  configuring 59
index 243
index server 232
information composer
  about 113
  data, cleansing 114
  data columns, classifying 115
  data, loading 113, 114
  data, saving into SAP HANA 115
  data source, selecting 113, 114
  data, uploading 113
Information Design Tool (IDT) 127
information views
  Analytic View 24
  Attribute View 24
  Calculation View 24
  features 24
information views, composing
  about 116
  data, combining 116, 117
  data, refining 117
  data sources, selecting 116
In-Memory DataStore Object (IMDSO) 71
inner, join type 88
input parameters
  creating 179-181
  URL 181

J

JavaScript perspective 10
job
  creating 65
  executing 68
join 100, 116
join type
  full 88
  inner 88
  left outer 88
  referential 88
  right outer 88
  text 88

K

Kerberos authentication 201

L

left outer, join type 88
leveled hierarchy 174, 175
Lifecycle Management perspective 9
Link with Editor option 15
LM-structure 233
logging tables 53

M

Massive Parallel Processing (MPP) 218, 234
metadata
  importing, from SAP HANA Studio 60-63
metadata manager 238
Microsoft Excel
  URL 164
  used, for creating reports 158-164
model details 111, 112
Modeler perspective
  about 8, 22, 23
  diagram 23
  information views 24
  SQL Script 24
model list 112
multi-version concurrency control
    (MVCC) 238
My Data 118
My Information Views 118

N

name server 232
Navigator Pane
  administration 12
  Find System option 14
  Find Table option 14
  Link with Editor option 15
  SQL Console option 12, 13
  system, monitoring 12
  used, for SAP HANA Studio navigation 10, 11

O

OLAP
  about 250
  engine 93

SAP BusinessObjects Analysis, used for
    creating reports 154-156
Online Transactional Processing (OLTP) 250
Open Perspective 9

P

package
  creating 86
package privileges 203
page manager 241
parent-child hierarchy 176
persisted segment 243
persistence layer 241 238, 247, 248
PlanViz perspective 10
Plugin perspective 10
preprocessor server 232
presentation layer 210
privileges
  about 202
  analytic privileges 203
  package privileges 203
  SQL privileges 203
  system privileges 203
procedures
  creating, SQLScript used 184, 185
project
  creating 64
  saving 68
projection 100

Q

Query as a Web Service (QAWS) 138

R

Random Access Memory (RAM) 235
read module 53
referential, join type 88
reporting layer 122
reporting tools
  connecting, to SAP HANA 123-127
  URL 127
reports
  creating, Microsoft Excel used 158-164

creating, SAP BusinessObjects Analysis for OLAP used 154-157

creating, SAP BusinessObjects Dashboards used 148-153

creating, SAP BusinessObjects Explorer used 142-147

creating, SAP BusinessObjects Web I ntelligence used 128-141

creating, SAP Lumira used 165-168

Resource perspective 10

right outer, join type 88

roles

assigning, to users 193, 194

creating 192

row-based store engine 236

S

SAP 253

SAP BO Explorer. *See* **SAP BusinessObjects Explorer**

SAP BusinessObjects Analysis

URL 158

used, for creating reports 154-157

SAP BusinessObjects Dashboards

used, for creating reports 148-153

SAP BusinessObjects Explorer

about 93

configuration, connecting to 126

URL 148

used, for creating reports 142-147

SAP BusinessObjects Web Intelligence (SAP BO WebI)

used, for creating reports 128-141

SAP Business Suite

on SAP HANA 256, 257

SAP BWA

and SAP HANA, comparing 229, 230

SAP Data Services

about 27

benefits 68

datastore, creating in 56, 57

key factors 27

table, importing in 58

using, for data provisioning 55

using, for data provisioning 68, 69

vs, SLT and Sybase replication 29, 30

SAP DS Version 4.0 55

SAP ERP

URL 258

SAP HANA

about 205, 220

advantages 221

analytic privileges, creating 195-200

and SAP BWA, comparing 229, 230

applications 253, 254

architecture 231-233

column-based store engine 236

currency conversion 172-174

databases versus traditional databases 221-223

data, saving into 115

data storage 219, 220

evolution 229

features 224-228

logging, securing 200-203

log storage 219

RAM 219

reporting layer 122

reporting tools, connecting 123-127

roles, assigning to users 193, 194

roles, creating 192

row-based store engine 236

SAP Business Suite 256, 257

SAP in-memory computing engine 226

SAP NetWeaver BW 218, 254-256

server 219

software update 233

traditional versus in-memory 221-223

URL 90

users, creating 189-191

view, saving to 117

SAP HANA Cloud

URL 110

SAP HANA Development perspective 8

SAP HANA DXC Implementation Guide

URL 75

SAP HANA modeling

about 83-85

URL 85

SAP HANA Studio

about 6, 84

Eclipse perspectives 7

installation paths 7
metadata, importing from 60-63
navigating, Navigator Pane used 10, 11
supported platform 6
system requirements 6
SAP HANA Studio repository 233
SAP HANA system
datastore, creating for 64
source file, selecting 34, 35
table, creating 31-33
target table, selecting 34, 35
SAP Host Agent 233
SAP in-memory computing engine 225
SAP Landscape Transformation. *See* **SLT**
SAP Lumira
reports, creating in 165-167
URL 110, 169
SAP NetWeaver BW
about 218
by SAP HANA 254-256
technical requisites 218, 219
URL 256
SAP NetWeaver Version 7.0 73
SAP Solution Manager diagnostic agent 233
SAP Solution Manager (SAP SOLMAN) 233
**Security Assertion Markup Language
       (SAML) 190**
segments 241
Sidecar approach 74
SLT
about 26
components 52
configuration 42-50
key factors 26
using, for data provisioning 41, 51-54
vs, SAP Data Services and Sybase replication
       29, 30
SLT, components
control module 52
logging tables 52
read module 52
write module 52
source file
selecting, in SAP HANA system 34, 35
SQL Console option 12, 13
SQL privileges 203

SQLScript
about **24**
used, for creating calculation view 104, 106
used, for creating procedures 184, 185
Standalone HANA. *See* **Enterprise HANA**
static list 181
statistics server 232
SUSE Linux Enterprise Server (SLES) 219
Sybase replication
about 27
configuring 76-78
connection, creating 78, 79
key factors 27
setup, prerequisites 75, 76
testing 79, 80
using, for data provisioning 75, 81, 82
vs, SLT and SAP Data Services 29, 30
Sybase Replication Server 15.7.1 SP100
URL 82
**Sybase Replication Server Version 15.7.1
       SP100 75**
System Information tab 21
System Monitor option 12
system privileges 203

T

table
creating, in SAP HANA system 31-33, 55
importing, in SAP Data Services 58
target table
selecting, in SAP HANA system 34, 35
Team Synchronizing perspective 10
technology
about 211
data compression 215
multicore CPUs 213, 215
parallel processing 215
text, join type 88
Text Retrieval and Extraction (TREX) 243
traditional databases
about 206-208
architecture 210
bottlenecks 208
cost 209, 210
latency 208, 209

transactional version memory 241
transaction manager 237, 238

U

union 100, 117
universe
  creating, IDT used 128-130
users
  creating 189-191
  roles, assigning 193, 194

V

values
  changing 115
  merging 114
variables
  creating 177-179
  URL 179
Version Memory Consolidation 241
view
  My Data 118
  My Information Views 118
  saving, to SAP HANA 117, 118
Volumes tab 20

W

Web Intelligence (WebI)
  document creating, universe used 136-138
  URL 141
Window menu 9
workflow
  creating 66
write module 53
write operations 242

X

Xcelsius. *See* SAP BusinessObjects
      Dashboards
XS Engine 232

Thank you for buying
SAP HANA Cookbook

About Packt Publishing

Packt, pronounced 'packed', published its first book "*Mastering phpMyAdmin for Effective MySQL Management*" in April 2004 and subsequently continued to specialize in publishing highly focused books on specific technologies and solutions.

Our books and publications share the experiences of your fellow IT professionals in adapting and customizing today's systems, applications, and frameworks. Our solution-based books give you the knowledge and power to customize the software and technologies you're using to get the job done. Packt books are more specific and less general than the IT books you have seen in the past. Our unique business model allows us to bring you more focused information, giving you more of what you need to know, and less of what you don't.

Packt is a modern, yet unique publishing company, which focuses on producing quality, cutting-edge books for communities of developers, administrators, and newbies alike. For more information, please visit our website: www.PacktPub.com.

About Packt Enterprise

In 2010, Packt launched two new brands, Packt Enterprise and Packt Open Source, in order to continue its focus on specialization. This book is part of the Packt Enterprise brand, home to books published on enterprise software – software created by major vendors, including (but not limited to) IBM, Microsoft and Oracle, often for use in other corporations. Its titles will offer information relevant to a range of users of this software, including administrators, developers, architects, and end users.

Writing for Packt

We welcome all inquiries from people who are interested in authoring. Book proposals should be sent to author@packtpub.com. If your book idea is still at an early stage and you would like to discuss it first before writing a formal book proposal, contact us; one of our commissioning editors will get in touch with you.

We're not just looking for published authors; if you have strong technical skills but no writing experience, our experienced editors can help you develop a writing career, or simply get some additional reward for your expertise.

Software Development on the SAP HANA Platform

ISBN: 978-1-84968-940-3   Paperback: 328 pages

Unlock the true potential of the SAP HANA platform

1. Learn SAP HANA from an expert

2. Go from installation and setup to running your own processes in a matter of hours

3. Cover all the advanced implementations of SAP HANA to help you truly become a HANA master

Instant SAP HANA Starter

ISBN: 978-1-84968-868-0   Paperback: 66 pages

Everything you need to know to be able to build your first SAP HANA standalone application!

1. Learn something new in an Instant! A short, fast, focused guide delivering immediate results

2. Understand key principles behind SAP HANA

3. Discover the main features of the SAP HANA Studio for application design

4. Create a reporting application on the SAP HANA platform

Please check **www.PacktPub.com** for information on our titles

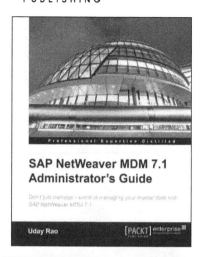

**SAP NetWeaver MDM 7.1
Administrator's Guide**

ISBN: 978-1-84968-214-5   Paperback: 336 pages

Don't just manage — excel at managing your master data
with SAP NetWeaver MDM 7.1

1. Written in an easy-to-follow manner, and in
   simple language

2. Step-by-step procedures that take you from basic to
   advanced administration of SAP MDM in no time

3. Learn various techniques for effectively
   managing master data using SAP MDM 7.1
   with illustrative screenshots

**SAP ABAP Advanced
Cookbook**

ISBN: 978-1-84968-488-0   Paperback: 316 pages

Over 80 advanced recipes with excellent programming
techniques that focus on the Netweaver 7.0 EHP2
and above

1. Full of illustrations, diagrams, and tips with clear
   step-by-step instructions and real-time examples

2. Get to grips with solving complicated problems
   using Regular Expressions in ABAP

3. Master the creation of common Design Patterns
   using ABAP Objects

4. Enhance SAP applications through the use of
   ABAP programming

Please check **www.PacktPub.com** for information on our titles